Seeds

Andrew Mikolajski

Seeds

photographs by Deirdre Rooney

MARABOUT

Introduction

Growing plants from seed is always rewarding. It seems almost incredible that a tiny seed can so readily be persuaded to burst into life and push out roots, shoots and leaves to create a new plant.

We all love flowers, but seasoned gardeners come to appreciate the whole plant and keep a close eye on its annual life cycle, from the moment it puts out fresh growth in spring until it gets ready for a well-deserved rest in autumn. For them, the process of seed production is a fascinating one, once they realise its importance to a plant's survival. The majority of seed cases often have a unique and subtle beauty of their own. Their appeal goes way beyond the aesthetic – while a flower is transient, a seed case is literally full of potential for a whole new generation of plants. And a garden that is full of seeds will be as much a haven for wildlife as one that is full of flowers.

Growing plants from seed is such a natural process it is surprising how few gardeners regularly attempt it. Yes, most of us grow annuals and few vegetables each year, but it takes only a moment's thought to realise that a vast range of plants beyond these can also be grown from seed – perennials, shrubs, even trees and conifers.

This book is a guide to the techniques involved in collecting seed, sowing it, getting it to sprout and growing on the resulting seedlings. If you are beginner, start with a few easy vegetables or annuals, for which packeted seed is readily available. These are generally easy to grow. Put a few beans in the ground in late winter and you will be feeding your family and filling the freezer within months. Then get outdoors in autumn and start harvesting seed from the plants in your garden – and begging seed from the gardens of neighbours and friends. No good gardener ever refuses. You could even try sowing the seed of fruits in your weekly shopping basket – the results might surprise you...

what is a seed?

A seed is a plant waiting to happen. It is nothing short of miraculous that a tiny seed – actually an embryonic plant – contains all the information necessary to create a huge tree (or even a short-lived weed). All that is required to persuade a seed to burst into life is warmth, moisture and light.

How plants grow

Plants are permanently adolescent. Unlike us, they don't reach a point at which they stop growing. Every year they put out fresh growth – new shoots, leaves and flowers (the flowers being designed to attract pollinators).

Pollination occurs when pollen grains, which produce male sex cells, from one flower are transferred onto the stigma, holding the female sex cells, of another. Seed production is sexual, but it's sex by surrogacy, usually as a result of insect activity though it can also happen when pollen is transferred from plant to plant on the wind. Fertilisation then occurs, the flower fades and seed is formed.

Seed cases

Seeds are held in a fruit, the part of the plant that develops after pollination. Strictly, the term 'fruit' has a much broader sense than the one generally used to refer to edible fruits, as it applies to any seed case.

There are various types of fruit. **Pome fruits** are firm but not woody and contain several seeds. These include the apples and pears and a number of ornamentals. **Drupes** are fleshy and contain a stone, itself containing one or more seeds. Peaches, plums and apricots are all drupes, sometimes also called **stone fruits**. A vast number of ornamental trees and shrubs produce their seed in fleshy **berries**. (Berry is the term loosely applied to any fleshy fruit that contains one or more seeds.)

Some plants produce seeds in cases that dry out and split to release the seeds. The legumes (Leguminosae) are a large family of plants that produce seeds in elongated **pods** that dry out then split – all the peas and beans, plus many ornamentals such as laburnums, lupins and sweet peas belong to this family. **Cones**, produced by the conifers, are usually woody structures that split open to release their seeds. This list is not exhaustive.

How seeds disperse

Plants do not have powers of locomotion and need to rely on outside agencies to disperse their seed. From their point of view, it's in their best interests if the seed can be spread over as wide an area as possible. Plants have evolved a number of strategies that enable this to happen.

The most primitive method of seed dispersal is on the wind. Dust-like seed is easily blown about. Other seeds have papery wings or bits of fluff clinging to them that improve aerodynamics. It's no coincidence that in many parts of the world the shedding of seed coincides with blustery weather. Just think of the storms that commonly occur in autumn and early winter. Shedding seed at this time of year is the best method of ensuring the widest possible distribution of potential offspring.

CLOCKWISE FROM TOP LEFT *Drupe (apricot); cone (pine); pyracantha berries; pod (wisteria); pome (chaenomeles); clematis seedhead.*

Seed comes in all different sizes.

time the seed is ejected in a pile of manure some distance from the parent plant.

In practice, the majority of seeds seldom wind up in situations that encourage germination and growth. Hence plants tend to produce seed in vast quantities. This is good for gardeners.

Dormancy and viability

All seed is dormant. Only specific conditions will trigger it into life. For a seed to sprout it has to be ripe and the environmental conditions have to be right. Strangely, seed contains chemicals that actually inhibit germination, and/or have protective coatings that prevent germination occurring. Actually, this is vital for the long-term survival of the species. Many seeds can stay dormant for years, waiting for the right conditions for germination to occur. Seed that is capable of germinating is described as viable.

It's a matter of the survival of the species. If local conditions change radically and all the plants belonging to a particular species die out, hopefully seed will have landed somewhere else where conditions are more favourable.

For seed that is enclosed inside a fruit, there are two possible scenarios. Either some animal or bird bites into it, finds it unpalatable and spits it out, or eats the fruit, chewing the seed in the process. Seeds can't be digested, so in the fullness of

The seed of certain plants, however, usually that of annuals, remains viable only in the short term. Seed packets are usually stamped with a 'sow by' date. If this passes you can still sow the seed, but in all probability only a small percentage will germinate.

Species, cultivars and hybrids

A species is a plant found growing in the wild. The names of species are always styled in italics, such as *Berberis darwinii*. All species can be grown from seed.

Seedlings raised in cultivation occasionally show distinguishing features and are referred to as selected forms or cultivars – shorthand for 'cultivated variety'. *Berberis darwinii* 'Flame' is in most respects similar to the species, but has broader leaves and more richly coloured flowers. If you collect seed from this, however, the resulting seedlings will probably resemble the wild plant – not 'Flame'.

Some species will hybridise with each other. *Berberis* x *lologensis* – the 'x' signalling it is a hybrid – arose as a cross between *Berberis darwinii* and *Berberis linearifolia*. Take seed from this and the seedlings will be of one or other of the parents. Hybrids cannot be grown from seed.

Plant breeders create new plants by systematically crossing species and hybrids. You'll recognise such plants by their names, which comprise a single Latin word followed by a name in inverted commas, eg *Rosa* 'Queen Elizabeth'. These also cannot be raised from seed.

Genetic variability

Some plant species show great genetic stability. In practice, this means that all the plants that develop from seed look similar, indeed may be virtually indistinguishable from each other. Others are less stable, and seedlings can show considerable variation in the size of the plant, flower colour and even non-visible factors such as hardiness and resistance to disease. This is what makes growing from seed so exciting. You can never be entirely sure what the results will be in many cases. The lenten hellebore, *Helleborus orientalis*, for instance, can produce seedlings with a wide colour range – white, cream, pink, cherry red and purple – and the first flowers are always keenly anticipated.

Strains

For plants that have a short life – annuals in other words – it's possible to isolate genes and to consolidate certain desirable characteristics by repeatedly crossing the plants that show them. While the species remains variable, certain strains that show relative uniformity have been produced by careful selection and dedicated breeding programmes by seed producers. For instance, the familiar tobacco plant *Nicotiana* x *sanderae* was produced by crossing *N. alata* and *N. forgetiana*. The flowers of this cross can be red, pink, purple or white. Careful breeding within the group has isolated dwarf strains and others that produce flowers of one colour.

F1 and F2 hybrids

You'll often see packets of annual seeds labelled F1 – less commonly F2 – hybrids. F1 hybrids are produced by crossing two selected parents that have both been systematically inbred to produce a strain of considerable uniformity. Although these are more expensive than ordinary seeds, they are well worth the extra expense, particularly if you are new to growing from seed. They germinate readily and give much better results.

F2 hybrids are produced by crossing F1 plants with themselves or another seed strain. The resulting seedlings will not be quite as uniform or vigorous as F1 hybrids.

Germination

A seedling's emergence is a complex process, most of which takes place below ground so is unseen by the gardener.

As the seed takes up water, it swells and the seed coat breaks down. First to appear is a primary root, known as the radicle. Then the seed leaves, or cotyledons, emerge. These do not resemble those of the mature plant, and may not even appear above the ground. They function only as a food reserve that helps keep the embryonic plant alive. Following these, the first true leaves appear.

LEFT *An ungerminated bean.* RIGHT *The first leaf emerges shortly after the radicle.*

tools and equipment

While some seed can be germinated and grown on outdoors (see Collecting, preparing and sowing seed, page 27), most gardeners prefer to raise new plants from seed in controlled conditions, using the equipment detailed below.

Containers

A wide range of container types is suitable for seed sowing. Terracotta pots were long the material of choice, but have nowadays been superseded by plastic. Plastic has the distinct advantage of lightness, plus it is really easy to wash – an important matter, as young seedlings can be vulnerable to disease and so good hygiene is important.

You can use either small pots or trays. If you want to raise only a few plants, use pots. Don't be tempted to use too large a pot, as you'll create a sump of compost at the bottom of the pot that the seedling roots won't reach down to. Trays are useful when you are sowing fine seeds in quantity. Modules are best for seeds that are large enough to be sown singly.

Paper or peat pots can be useful as roots can grow through the sides, so you know exactly when the seedling is ready for potting on or planting up. You don't have to knock the plant out of the peat pot, just pot it on as it is. The pot rapidly rots down. These are particularly useful for seedlings that resent root disturbance. However they tend to dry out easily, so have to be kept well watered. That's not so good for bulbs and other plants that appreciate swift drainage so, for these, stick to plastic.

Tall, narrow pots, sometimes called long toms, paper tubes and long modules are designed for plants with long root systems or taproots. Sweet peas, tomatoes and other seedlings that rapidly develop deep roots are often started in these. Ordinary pots can be used, however, so it is not always essential to purchase long toms.

Composts

Most gardeners use a multi-purpose soil-less compost for everything – container plants, hanging baskets, cuttings as well as seed sowing. These composts, which are cheap and widely available, are excellent, but they do have limitations. Most are based on peat. Leaving aside the environmental issue – that peat is not a renewable resource – peat as a growing medium tends to hold on moisture. This is not generally a problem for most seeds, but can lead to problems with damping off (see Seedling problems, page 189). And seeds that are slow to germinate can rot off. Peat is not a good choice for seeds of drought-loving plants such as cacti, alpines and most species from the Mediterranean and Middle East. Coir-based composts, usually recommended to peat-haters, tend to be, if anything, even more moisture-retentive. You can alleviate this potential problem by mixing these composts with horticultural grit, perlite or vermiculite – use one part of any of these to three parts of compost.

Many gardeners prefer soil-based composts, which produce more reliable results, but where this is recommended in the pages that follow soil-less compost

CLOCKWISE FROM TOP LEFT *Plastic trays and peat pots; modules; perlite, vermiculite, grit, compost; modules and tubes that are suitable for sweet peas.*

can be substituted. Soil-based composts are heavier and more free draining than the multi-purpose types. They are usually made up to a specific formula, as defined by the John Innes Institute. You will probably come across John Innes seed compost, but failing that use a John Innes No.1. Again, though, you can add horticultural grit, perlite or vermiculite, just to improve drainage.

Seed composts are low in nutrients. When potting on, choose the compost appropriate to the type of plant. Use John Innes No.1 or No.2 for annuals, No.2 for perennials and bulbs and No.3 for trees and shrubs. Add grit, perlite or vermiculite for growing on bulbs and other plants that appreciate good drainage.

Propagators

While you can raise many plants outdoors or on a kitchen windowsill, if you want to make an early start to your sowing and grow a wide range of plants it is worth investing in a propagator. In essence, this is a closed case that provides a warm, humid environment that speeds up seed germination and seedling growth. Quick growth after germination is important if you are going to avoid damping off (see Seedling problems, page 189).

If you are raising just a few seeds in pots, you can simply tent each pot with a clear plastic bag. Some seed trays are sold with clear plastic covers that fit over the top. Keeping the cover over the tray raises the humidity and the temperature, but only by a few degrees. This means they are best used from early spring onwards when only a slight hike in temperature is necessary to get seeds to germinate. You can place these trays near a heat source, such as just above a radiator, but as this heat tends to be directional you need to keep turning the tray to ensure even heat distribution.

The other alternative is to invest in a heated propagator. These contain an element in the base and are plugged into the mains. Often the lids have vents so you can regulate the temperature. More sophisticated models have thermostatic controls. These are a good investment if you are growing a lot of tender plants that need high temperatures over several weeks for the seeds to germinate.

Cold frames

A cold frame is like a mini-greenhouse about 1m (3ft) square or larger, either made of brick or timber with a glass or sturdy, clear plastic lid. Some models are entirely glazed. A cold frame is designed to protect seedlings and other young plants from frost. It can also provide a suitable environment for germinating the seeds of hardy plants.

Site a cold frame in a sheltered area outdoors, out of direct sunlight that could scorch tender young plant growth. Butted up to the house or a greenhouse wall is usually ideal.

Labels

Whenever you sow a batch of seedlings, label them with the name of the plant and the date of sowing. This is especially important if you are raising a lot of different plants. Many seedlings look almost identical, and the date is vital for those seeds that are slow to germinate. Only admit defeat when you are certain those seeds are not going to sprout.

Dibbers

A dibber is a neat little bit of kit that is far more useful than you would think possible. For making holes in compost for larger seeds you could use a pencil or chopstick, but once you are transplanting seeds outdoors you'll soon realise how a dibber comes into its own. It is the ideal tool for making holes of the appropriate width and depth at the quickest rate.

Soil thermometer

A soil thermometer is useful if you are sowing seed outdoors after a cold spell in early spring and you want to make sure the soil is warm enough. Knowing the soil temperature is by no means critical, though, as any seed sown when it's too cool will simply wait for the weather to warm up before sprouting.

A soil thermometer is perhaps most useful when you are growing seedlings under glass and you need to check that the compost temperature is high enough for germination and good seedling growth.

Fertilisers

If you are growing seedlings on in containers for longer than four to six weeks you will need to feed them, as any nutrients in the compost will be used up. Use a general-purpose fertiliser – these are best applied in liquid form as a root drench every two to three weeks. On young seedlings, apply the fertiliser at half strength. For vegetable crops you can substitute organic fertilisers based on seaweed. For trees, shrubs and climbers that are kept in their containers for two years or more, it can be more timesaving to substitute a granular slow-release fertiliser, lightly forked into the compost surface. Apply the fertiliser at the start of the growing season in early spring, providing a top-up in early to midsummer.

For plants you want to bring into flower quickly, such as annuals, use a tomato fertiliser, which will have the right level of potassium to boost flower production.

TOP TO BOTTOM *Seed tray with cover; labels are vital; a soil thermometer and dibber.*

collecting, preparing and sowing seed

Left to their own devices, plants seed themselves around without human intervention. Gardeners, however, love being in control, and want to speed up the process of germination and make their own choices as to what's going to survive – and what isn't.

Buying seed

Seeds of annuals, biennials and vegetables are widely available in garden centres, DIY stores and even supermarkets. For the widest choice, however, refer to seed catalogues. Most seed merchants introduce new varieties every year, and ordering by post is the way to ensure you'll get the best of what's available. Seed of new varieties is likely to be in short supply, so you may need to order in advance.

Some perennial seed is also available to purchase, though less widely. You'll be hard pressed to find the seed of trees and shrubs in any garden centre, however. There are specialist seed merchants who sell seed and some allotment societies and gardening clubs have seed swaps. You can also do searches on the Internet.

Collecting seed

Far more rewarding, and much cheaper, than buying seed is collecting it yourself.

Is it worth it?

The short answer is yes, but not all seed you find in gardens is worth sowing. If the plant is a species, go ahead. If it is a selected form, you can collect and sow seed but the seedlings will not be the same as the parent plant. Depending on the size of the gene pool, you will either get a plant such as the ones you see in the wild, or a form of it (see Species, cultivars and hybrids, page 10). It is not worth collecting seed from hybrid plants with complex parentage. This includes not only many annuals, but also most roses, camellias, rhododendrons and narcissi.

To deadhead or not to deadhead

Normally, it's considered good garden practice to remove faded flowers before seed is formed. This encourages the plant either to produce further flowers or to invest its energies in growing new stems that will flower the following year. Seed production, from the plant's point of view, is an exhausting process. In the case of annuals, it actually hastens the death of the plant.

To prevent too many tragedies in the garden, be selective. If there's a plant, or group of plants, that you want seed from, you need only leave a few flowers to complete their cycle and remove the rest. Seed is usually produced in copious amounts. The exception here is the plants that produce colourful berries that are decorative in their own right as well as providing a much-needed food source for birds in winter – cotoneasters, berberis, pyracanthas and rowans, for example. In such cases, trim back some of the new growth in midsummer so that the berries are exposed to the sun to ripen fully.

Harvesting seed

Seed cases and fruits should be allowed to develop fully on the plant before they are removed, or the seed will not be completely ripe.

Collecting seed from seed cases

For seed cases that dry out as the seed ripens, the cases should be just starting to split, or be about to split. This can be any time from midsummer onwards, depending on when the plant flowered and how hot and dry the weather is following flowering.

1 Cut flowered stems from the plant as they begin to dry out. The seedhead here was taken from *Iris sibirica*.

2 Put the seedhead in a brown paper bag, then hang it upside down in a warm airy place such as a kitchen so that it can dry out fully. As the cases split open the seeds will be caught in the bag.

Extracting seed from fleshy berries

Berries should be harvested only when they are fully ripe, usually from mid- to late autumn. Wait until after the first frosts if possible, as this will help break down the fleshy outer coating. You need to extract the seeds from the berries if you want to sow them.

1   Cut clusters of berries from the plant when they are fully ripe and squashy, usually not before mid-autumn. The berries shown in the pictures here are from a pyracantha.

2   Squash the berries between your finger and thumb to release the seeds.

3   Wash the seeds in tepid water to remove all traces of the fruit.

4   Dry the seeds on absorbent kitchen paper. They are then ready for further treatment, for sowing or for storing (see storing seed, page 23).

Breaking dormancy

The act of sowing seed is often sufficient to break a seed's dormancy. But the seeds of many hardy plants need treatment first to initiate or speed up germination.

Stratification

The seeds of some plants need exposure to cold, usually 0.5–5°C (33–41°F), to break their dormancy. If you live in a cold area, simply sow the seed as normal then place the containers outdoors. This does not guarantee a sufficient length of time at the appropriate temperature, however. To increase the likelihood of germination, mix the seed with moistened peat, perlite or vermiculite in a clear plastic bag, label with the plant name and date and place in the refrigerator. Start checking the bag after four weeks. If the seeds are sprouting, sow them as described on page 25. Return seeds that have failed to germinate to the fridge.

Most seed requires a chilling time of six to eight weeks, though this may need to be extended to twelve. Sow all the seed after twelve weeks, whether it has germinated in the fridge or not.

Soaking

You can break the dormancy of the seed of certain leguminous plants, such as

Storing seed

Most seed is best sown fresh, but you can usually store it and it will remain dormant. Seed for storing must be dry and be kept dry. Small paper envelopes are suitable, as are glass screwtop jars. Keep the seed somewhere cool and dark – the salad drawer in the refrigerator is an ideal place.

TOP *Stratification – seed mixed with perlite.*
BOTTOM *Soaking leguminous seeds.*

lupins and sweet peas, by soaking the seeds in hot, but not boiling, water for 24 hours before sowing them. Make sure you do not soak them for any longer, however, as this can lead to the seed rotting.

Soaking is not always necessary, but if you are collecting seed after a long, hot, dry summer, the seed coat may well be tougher than normal.

Scarification

Some seed has a tough outer coating that actually acts as a physical barrier preventing the seed from taking up water and germinating. Chestnuts (*Castanea*) are a familiar example. Scarification is the method used to break down the coating.

You can breach the seed coat in a number of ways. Nicking the seed coat with a sharp knife is the best method for large seed such as acorns. Take care not to damage the embryo inside, however. You can also scarify seeds by rubbing them between sheets of sandpaper so that the coating is scratched. Another method is to mix the seed with a small quantity of sharp sand. Place this in a screwtop jar and shake vigorously. These methods are suitable for plants with small seeds that are tricky to handle individually.

Seed abraded by any of these methods can then be sown as described opposite.

When to sow

Most seed that you collect yourself is best sown immediately. However, since it may not germinate until spring, some gardeners like to store it over winter.

Traditionally, spring is the time for sowing annuals, but there is an increasing number of gardeners who like to sow in the autumn. This policy slightly increases the workload, because you have to protect the young plants over winter, but brings certain positive benefits. It's possible to produce sturdy plants for planting out earlier the following spring and you can also enjoy some salad crops throughout

Sowing *in situ*

This basically means sowing seeds where you want them to grow. This method is usually used for vegetable crops and occasionally for ornamentals.

Prepare the site by digging it over with a fork and removing all large stones and traces of weeds. Break down clods of soil with the back of the fork. You can improve the soil by digging in garden compost or well-rotted farmyard manure. Increase soil fertility by forking in a general-purpose, slow-release garden fertiliser in granular form. Rake the surface level.

Vegetables are usually sown in rows. Mark out the rows with canes or by stretching strings between short pegs. Depending on the size of the seed, you can either surface sow or mark out a shallow furrow with the back of a rake.

Assuming you are using bought seed, the packet tells you how far apart the adult plants should be. If the seeds are large enough to be handled easily, sow them at the appropriate distance. Rather than guess, you can either stretch a tape measure the length of the drill or mark off the distances on a cane or length of bamboo that you lay next to the drill as a guide.

If the seed is very fine, hold the seed in one cupped hand then take a pinch of seed with the index finger and thumb of the other. Sprinkle the seed thinly along the row. Seedlings must be thinned to the recommended distance when they are large enough to handle. Don't leave them closer together, however healthy they may look, as they will crowd each other out.

the winter. The trick is to keep the plants at a temperature high enough to stop them dying back but not so high that they produce significant growth, which tends to be weak and disease prone.

There is hardly a season of the year when you could not be sowing seed. However, there are peaks in spring and autumn and troughs in summer and winter.

Sowing seed

Fill pots or trays with the appropriate compost and tamp this down lightly to level the surface. Water thoroughly – the aim is to moisten the whole volume of the compost, not just the surface, without flooding it, which can compact the material. Water either with a watering can fitted with a fine rose or stand the containers in a bowl of shallow water and allow the compost to become wet by capillary action. The compost surface should be evenly moist. Drain the containers thoroughly before sowing the seed.

As a rule of thumb, seed should be covered with compost to its own depth. If the seeds are reasonably large, such as nasturtium seeds, you can make holes in the compost with a dibber, drop in the seeds and draw the surrounding compost over. Alternatively, lightly press the seeds into the compost surface then top them with a layer of fresh compost so they are buried to the right depth.

Small seed can be surface sown. Sprinkle on the seed, lightly press it down to ensure good adhesion with the compost, then dust over a light covering of compost. Actually it's usually easier to sprinkle over a light layer of vermiculite.

TOP TO BOTTOM *Nick the tough coats of seeds such as chestnuts with a knife; large leguminous seeds can be rubbed with sandpaper; shake smaller seeds with sharp sand in a screwtop jar.*

If the seed is small and dark in colour you may not be able to see it clearly against the compost. Vermiculite is easy to see.

Water the pots again from above, with a can fitted with a fine rose, or mist them with a spray. Allow them to drain before moving them. You won't need to water the seeds again until they germinate. To raise the temperature around the seeds and encourage them to germinate, put the pots or containers in a propagator or cold frame as appropriate. You can tent individual pots with a clear plastic bag. Annuals sown in late spring or early summer can usually be germinated outside.

Pricking out

There are few more exciting sights than the first leaves emerging from the compost. At this preliminary stage, the seedlings are far too small and delicate to handle. However, once the second set of leaves has appeared you can prick them out. First prepare fresh pots or trays filled with the appropriate compost, water this well, then allow them to drain. Holding the seedlings by the leaves, gently pull them out of the compost. A dibber can be useful for teasing out the roots. Make holes in the fresh compost with the dibber and drop each seedling into place. Lightly firm them in with your fingers, then mist or water with a can fitted with a fine rose. The seedlings may wilt initially, but should soon perk up.

Some seedlings, such as sweet peas (*Lathyrus odoratus*), resent root disturbance so should be grown on where they are. Transplant them only when they are large enough for their final, flowering positions.

The hardiness of plants

Plants that can withstand temperatures below freezing are described as hardy. However, hardiness is relative and depends on the local climate. In a warm, sheltered garden, plants that would normally be expected to succumb during a hard winter can often survive unharmed.

- In this book, plants are assumed to tolerate several degrees of frost, apart from the ones dealt with in 'the indoor garden', all of which are tender. Also, some vegetables are not hardy, so the strategies necessary to grow them successfully outdoors in cool climates are described.

- Annuals are usually classified as hardy or half-hardy. Most of the former can be germinated in spring and kept outdoors. Half-hardy annuals should not be planted outside until all risk of frost has passed – usually late spring.

- All seedlings and young plants are susceptible to frost damage, even if the adults are hardy, so require some degree of protection over winter or during cold weather. This applies particularly to annuals and biennials sown in autumn.

- The seed of plants that are borderline hardy are usually best stored over winter and sown in spring, if you live in an area with cold winters. While they can be germinated in autumn, the seedlings are more vulnerable to frost damage than those of fully hardy plants so require extra protection.

Growing on

If you are growing your young plants on in compost, feeding will be necessary to keep them growing strongly and bring them to flowering size as quickly as possible. Although most composts contain fertiliser, the plant rapidly uses this up. It is therefore a good idea to use a fertiliser during the growing season.

As they are growing on keep the seedlings well watered and make sure they have adequate light. You may need to pot the seedlings on again before they are ready for planting out. The aim is to produce sturdy little plants that are well clothed with leaves. Annuals should normally be about 7.5cm (3in) tall, perennials up to 15cm (6in). Seedlings of woody plants are unlikely to be ready for planting out until they are about three years old.

Hardening off

If you have germinated your seedlings in a propagator, once they are growing strongly you need to get them used to the idea of life in the real world. Gradually lower the temperature, either by adjusting the thermostat – if there is one – or by opening the vents in the lid. After a few days of this, you can remove the lid altogether for increasingly longer periods. You'll soon be able to stand the pots outdoors in the daytime, bringing them in at night.

If you've germinated your seeds in containers outdoors, put them in a cold frame overnight and at any other times when frost is threatened. Keep them permanently in the frame if there's a sudden cold snap of a few days or more.

TOP *Parsley seedlings ready for pricking out.*
BOTTOM *Larger seedlings can be potted up individually and grown on.*

trees, shrubs and climbers

Berberis

Barberry Berberidaceae

These thorny shrubs, deciduous or evergreen, are excellent for hedging, most having a dense, compact habit and tolerant of regular clipping. The best ones provide two seasons of interest, the yellow or orange flowers in spring being followed by red or black autumn berries.

why grow from seed

Berberis hybridise easily with each other, and some interesting forms can emerge, so it's well worth extracting and sowing seed just to see what you get.

aftercare

Pot on the seedlings annually, using soil-based compost (John Innes No.3), or line them out in a nursery bed until they are large enough to plant out in their final positions. Water seedlings in containers and feed with a liquid fertiliser while they are in active growth from spring to summer, then overwinter them in a cold frame.

FAR RIGHT *Berberis berries ripen to red, as here, purple or bluish-black.*

1 Remove the berries from the stems in mid- to late autumn, preferably after they have been softened by the first frosts. Squash the berries to release the seeds, then wash them in water.

2 Dry the seeds on absorbent kitchen paper. They are then ready for sowing in pots outdoors. Alternatively, you can stratify them for four to six weeks in the fridge, then sow them in pots or trays of seed compost.

Cedrus atlantica

Blue Atlas cedar Pinaceae

WHEN TO SOW
Early spring.

PRE-TREATMENT
Stratify the seed in the fridge. You can also put some seed in the freezer, as the chilling requirement for germination can vary.

HOW TO SOW
In pots or trays of standard seed compost topped with grit.

GERMINATION
Seeds can be erratic to sprout but should germinate within two years.

TIME TILL FLOWERING
5 years.

ULTIMATE SIZE
40m x 10m (130ft x 33ft), but often less in cultivation.

This variable conifer hails from north Africa, though it is perfectly hardy. Surprisingly, in spite of its ultimate stature, many gardeners seem to have no compunction about planting it in quite small gardens, bowled over by the beauty of its cool blue foliage and cones. It makes a fine specimen in the short to medium term.

why grow from seed

Seed is probably the most reliable method of producing fresh stock of this plant. Seedlings can vary in the degree of blue in the leaf, so grow on only the ones with the best colour.

aftercare

Place the pots or trays outdoors. Pot on the seedlings annually into fresh compost (John Innes No.3) and keep them well watered during the growing season (spring to summer). Feed with a slow-release fertiliser at the start of each growing season. Young seedlings should be overwintered in a cold frame. Plant out in their final positions when large enough, which is usually not before they are five years old.

FAR RIGHT *Ripe cedar cones are the size of duck eggs and are slightly resinous.*

1 Remove mature, two-year-old cones from the tree, twisting them to break the union with the branch. If a cone is still closed soak it for 24 hours in warm water, or put it near a heat source such as a radiator.

2 After soaking, cones should start to open. Gently tap them on a hard surface and the seeds will emerge. Mix the seed with dampened perlite then seal in plastic bags. Place some in the fridge, others in the freezer, for three weeks. Sow in seed compost topped with grit.

Chaenomeles

Japonica, ornamental quince Rosaceae

WHEN TO SOW
Autumn.

PRE-TREATMENT
Stratify the seed before sowing.

HOW TO SOW
In pots or trays of standard
seed compost.

GERMINATION
4–6 months.

TIME TILL FLOWERING
3–5 years.

ULTIMATE SIZE
1.5m x 1.5m (5ft x 5ft), more if
wall-trained.

These are those lovely plants you sometimes notice in spring, when the bare stems are covered in sealing wax red flowers – or, more rarely, and less strikingly, white or pink. After the flowers come the fruits, hard, like miniature apples, and bright golden yellow. Attractive as freestanding shrubs, trained against a wall they are truly spectacular.

why grow from seed

If your plant has been tightly trained against a wall, there may be scant material available for taking cuttings. In this scenario, seed is the best option for making new plants.

aftercare

Pot the seedlings on annually into soil-based compost (John Innes No.3) until large enough to plant in their flowering positions. Water them regularly and feed with a liquid fertiliser while in active growth from spring to summer. Overwinter young plants in a cold frame. Remember that, like adult plants, they will shed their leaves each autumn.

FAR RIGHT *Chaenomeles fruits are like little yellow apples and almost as attractive as the spring flowers.*

1 Remove the fruits from the plant in mid- to late autumn after they have ripened from green. Cut the fruits in half with a sharp knife in order to expose the seeds.

2 Carefully remove the seeds with the tip of a knife. Discard any seeds you may have damaged when cutting the fruit. Stratify the seed for up to four weeks in the fridge before sowing in standard seed compost.

Clematis orientalis

Ranunculaceae

WHEN TO SOW
Autumn, when ripe; bought
seed can also be sown in spring.

PRE-TREATMENT
None necessary.

HOW TO SOW
Sow in pots or trays of standard
seed compost topped with grit
or sharp sand.

GERMINATION
8–12 weeks.

TIME TILL FLOWERING
2–3 years.

ULTIMATE SIZE
6m x 3m (20ft x 10ft), more or
less; the size can be restricted
with annual hard pruning in
late winter.

Clematis orientalis is an attractive plant,
covered in thick-petalled, bright yellow
lanterns from midsummer onwards. If you
buy packet seed of this plant, you'll see that
the feathery tails have been removed. If you
collect seed yourself, you can leave the tails
on. The similar *C. tangutica* and *C. tibetana*
can be treated in the same way.

why grow from seed
Since these plants have crossed with each other over many years,
interesting forms can arise. Some seedlings can produce flowers
whose petals flare dramatically outwards.

aftercare
Pot the seedlings on using a soil-based compost (John Innes No.3).
Feed with a liquid fertiliser and water them well when in active
growth from spring to summer. Stems will shrivel in winter, but
don't cut them back until the seedlings are well established.
Grow the seedlings on in containers, overwintering them in
a cold frame, until they are large enough to plant out.

FAR RIGHT *Clematis
seedheads are almost
as attractive as the
summer flowers.*

1 Remove seedheads
from the plant when
they are fully ripe – in
other words when they are
fluffy rather than silky.
Gently pull each seed away
from the seedhead.

2 Surface sow the seed
on pots or trays of seed
compost. A light topping
of fine grit or sharp sand will
help hold the seed in place.
Overwinter the containers in
a cold frame.

Colutea

Bladder senna Leguminosae

WHEN TO SOW
Sow in autumn, when ripe, or spring.

PRE-TREATMENT
Seed can either be soaked for 24 hours prior to sowing or rubbed with sandpaper.

HOW TO SOW
Sow in pots or trays of standard seed compost with added grit, sharp sand, perlite or vermiculite.

GERMINATION
2–4 weeks; autumn sowings may not germinate till the following spring.

TIME TILL FLOWERING
3–4 years.

ULTIMATE SIZE
2m x 2m (6½ft x 6½ft), or more.

This member of the pea family has species with yellow, orange or red flowers in summer that are followed by seed cases that puff up and become papery as they mature. Beware of harvesting the seed cases too early, before they are fully dry. Unripe seeds are white in colour but, in order to germinate, they should be dark.

why grow from seed

This plant can be raised from cuttings taken in summer, but, if you have missed the boat, try sowing some seed in autumn.

aftercare

Place the containers in a cold frame outdoors. You can speed up the germination of spring sowings by using a propagator at 15–18°C (59–64°F). Pot the seedlings on into soil-based compost (John Innes No.3) with added grit, sand, perlite or vermiculite. Water regularly and feed with a liquid fertiliser when in active growth from spring to summer. Overwinter the seedlings in a cold frame and plant out when two years old or more.

FAR RIGHT *By the time the seed pods are ripe the leaves will have withered and turned brown.*

1 Remove the inflated seed pods from the plant when they are dry and papery, but before they have split open.

2 Carefully break the pods along the seam to release the ripe seed, which should be dark in colour. Either sow the seed immediately or store over winter for sowing the following spring.

Cotoneaster horizontalis

Rosaceae

WHEN TO SOW
Sow in autumn.

PRE-TREATMENT
Stratify the seed before sowing.

HOW TO SOW
In trays or containers of standard seed compost.

GERMINATION
May take up to 18 months.

TIME TILL FLOWERING
3–4 years.

ULTIMATE SIZE
1m x 2m (3ft x 6½ft), or more.

This is a versatile plant with a stiff, herringbone habit. It looks good sprawling over a bank but can also be persuaded to ramp up a cool wall. The plant will be alive with bees when the small, dull white flowers froth up in late spring, and the vivid red autumn berries are a valuable food source for birds.

why grow from seed

This species has such a dense habit that suitable material for taking cuttings is not always easy to find. Fortunately, it is easily grown from seed, though you may need to be patient. All cotoneaster species can be raised from seed in the same way.

aftercare

Pot on the seedlings annually in soil-based compost (John Innes No.3). Water the seedlings and feed with a liquid fertiliser when in active growth in spring and summer. Overwinter them in a cold frame. Bear in mind that seedlings will lose their leaves in autumn just like adult plants. Plant out the seedlings in their final positions when two years old or more.

FAR RIGHT Cotoneaster berries ripen in autumn as the leaves are starting to change colour.

1 Cut the berries from the plant in mid- to late autumn, preferably after they have been softened by the first frosts. Squash the berries to release the seeds.

2 Wash the seeds in water, then dry them on absorbent kitchen paper. Mix them with dampened perlite or vermiculite in a plastic bag and place in the fridge for four to six weeks before sowing in standard seed compost.

Lathyrus latifolius

Perennial pea Leguminosae

WHEN TO SOW
Autumn to spring.

PRE-TREATMENT
Soak the seed for 24 hours, nick or rub with sandpaper before sowing.

HOW TO SOW
In pots or containers that can accommodate the long roots, which should be filled with standard seed compost.

GERMINATION
1–2 weeks; winter sowings may take longer.

TIME TILL FLOWERING
2–3 years.

ULTIMATE SIZE
2m x 2m (6½ft x 6½ft), or more.

Note the common name – perennial pea, not perennial sweet pea. These herbaceous climbers – they die back completely in winter – have all the beauty of the annuals, but alas not the scent. As well as the typical magenta, seed merchants have succeeded in isolating a desirable white form. You can train it formally, but it's pretty if just allowed to fling itself into the arms of a spring-flowering shrub.

why grow from seed

Plants do not divide easily, so seed is the simplest method of increasing your stocks of this plant. You can either collect seed from garden plants or buy packet seed.

aftercare

Once germinated, seedlings can be brought out of the cold frame by day. Return them when cold weather is forecast. Seedlings need cool conditions initially, or they will become leggy and the stems will be too soft. Water sparingly over winter, just to prevent the seedlings drying out. Once they perk up in spring, water frequently and feed with a general fertiliser. They should be large enough to plant out later the same year.

FAR RIGHT *The seeds of all* Lathyrus *species are held in pods that turn brown as they ripen.*

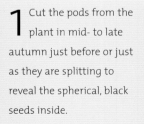
1 Cut the pods from the plant in mid- to late autumn just before or just as they are splitting to reveal the spherical, black seeds inside.

2 Soak the seeds in warm water for 24 hours to break down the seed coat and speed up germination. Soak only until the seed starts to swell, otherwise the seed can rot. Sow in pots or long toms and place in a cold frame outdoors.

Leycesteria formosa

Himalayan honeysuckle, pheasant berry Caprifoliaceae

WHEN TO SOW
Autumn.

PRE-TREATMENT
Stratify the seed outdoors.

HOW TO SOW
In pots or trays of standard seed compost topped with horticultural grit.

GERMINATION
8–12 weeks.

TIME TILL FLOWERING
3–5 years.

ULTIMATE SIZE
2m x 1.5m (6½ft x 5ft).

This rather sinister plant is valued for its late season. Its arching habit and racemes of dangling purplish red flowers make it suitable as a specimen or for the back of a border, but it also looks good in light woodland. The flowers are succeeded by berries of the same colour, so interest extends well into autumn.

why grow from seed

Cuttings of this plant do not always strike. Seed is a reliable method of increasing stocks.

aftercare

Place the containers outdoors. Once germinated, pot the seedlings on in containers filled with soil-based compost (John Innes No.3). Keep them well watered and feed with a liquid fertiliser when in active growth from spring to summer. Keep the seedlings in a cold frame over winter, when they will shed all their leaves. Plant them out in their final positions when they are two years old or more.

FAR RIGHT *Leycesteria berries are very soft and fleshy when ripe.*

1 Cut racemes of berries from the plant in mid- to late autumn when they are fully ripe and uniformly soft. Gently squash them to expose the seeds.

2 The seeds are tiny and difficult to handle, so the most practical strategy is to sow the crushed berries as they are, without trying to separate out the seeds. Top with horticultural grit to hold them in place on the compost surface.

Ligustrum

Privet Oleaceae

WHEN TO SOW
Winter.

PRE-TREATMENT
Stratify the seeds before sowing.

HOW TO SOW
In pots or trays filled with
standard seed compost.

GERMINATION
4–6 months.

TIME TILL FLOWERING
3–5 years.

ULTIMATE SIZE
2m x 2m (6½ft x 6½ft),
eventually if left unpruned.

An underestimated shrub if ever there was one, privet is still a popular choice as hedging. I would urge promoting it from that role. As a freestanding shrub it has a rare elegance, and its curiously scented panicles of dull white summer flowers will then develop as polished boot-blackened berries. The plant also makes a fetching standard, but regular clipping means you won't get those luscious-looking fruits.

why grow from seed

Most privets grown in gardens are species, so it is always worth collecting some seed if you are unable to take cuttings.

aftercare

Keep the containers outdoors until germinated. Pot the seedlings on and water and feed with a liquid fertiliser when in active growth from spring to autumn. Keep the containers in a cold frame over winter, when the leaves may be shed. Plant the seedlings out when they are two years old or more.

FAR RIGHT *Allowed to grow and flower without pruning, privets will berry in autumn.*

1 Harvest the berries when ripe in autumn and squash them to release the seeds. Be aware that the berries can stain.

2 Wash the seeds in water to clean off any bits of the fruit. Dry on absorbent kitchen paper, then mix with moistened perlite or vermiculite in a plastic bag. Put the seed in the fridge for three to four weeks. Sow in pots or trays filled with seed compost.

Lonicera

Honeysuckle, woodbine Caprifoliaceae

WHEN TO SOW
Autumn, when the seed is ripe.

PRE-TREATMENT
Stratify the seed before sowing.

HOW TO SOW
In pots or trays of standard
seed compost.

GERMINATION
4–6 months, sometimes longer.

TIME TILL FLOWERING
3–4 years.

ULTIMATE SIZE
3m x 3m (10ft x 10ft), or more;
prune to keep within bounds.

The scent of honeysuckle hanging on the air is one of those things that can sum up summer. It's usual to prune immediately after flowering, but if you leave a few flowered stems unpruned you will be able to harvest the seed in autumn.

why grow from seed
If a plant is too congested to provide good cuttings material, as can often happen, collect some seed instead.

aftercare
As the seedlings grow, the stems will start to twist. Push a thin cane into the compost to support them. To limit any potential damage to the roots, it is most practical to do this when potting the seedlings on. Water them regularly and feed with a liquid fertiliser when in active growth from spring to summer. Overwinter in a cold frame, at which time the leaves will be shed. Plant out when the seedlings are two years old or more.

FAR RIGHT *Honeysuckles are grown for their scented summer flowers, but they also produce attractive berries during autumn.*

1 Cut the berries from the plant in mid-autumn. Squash them to release the seeds, wash in water then dry them on absorbent paper. Mix the seed with moistened perlite or vermiculite and put in the fridge for three to four weeks.

2 Sow the seed in pots or trays of standard seed compost, then place the containers outdoors. Pot on the seedlings as they grow, using soil-based potting compost (John Innes No.3).

Malus

Crab apple Rosaceae

WHEN TO SOW
Autumn, when ripe.

PRE-TREATMENT
Stratify before sowing.

HOW TO SOW
In pots or trays of standard
seed compost.

GERMINATION
3–6 months.

TIME TILL FLOWERING
3–5 years.

ULTIMATE SIZE
10m x 8m (33ft x 26ft), more or
less, depending on the species.

Actually, you can sow the seed of any apple, even the ones you buy from a supermarket, to produce one of these lovely dainty trees that flower in mid-spring. All of them are beautiful. In autumn, enjoy the lovely mini-apples, which can be bright red or yellow among the turning leaves. The fruits usually hang on well after the leaves have changed colour and fallen.

why grow from seed

Nearly all crab apples are beautiful, so it's always worth sowing seed to produce a ready supply of ornamental plants.

aftercare

Place the containers outdoors. Once germinated, pot the seedlings on into soil-based compost (John Innes No.3). Water regularly and feed with a liquid fertiliser when in active growth in spring and summer. Keep in a cold frame over winter, when the leaves are shed. Plant out when two years old or more.

FAR RIGHT *Crab apples can be red, yellow or orange but are always eye-catching.*

1 Remove the fruits from the tree in mid- to late autumn, when fully ripe and showing an even colour. Cut the fruits in half to expose the seeds, which should be dark in colour. White seeds are not fully ripe.

2 With the tip of the knife, remove the seeds from the fruit. Throw away any damaged seed. Mix the seed with moistened perlite or vermiculite, seal in a plastic bag and place in the fridge for three to four weeks before sowing in pots or trays of standard seed compost.

Passiflora

Passion flower, granadilla Passifloraceae

WHEN TO SOW
Spring.

PRE-TREATMENT
None necessary.

HOW TO SOW
Sow in pots or trays of standard
seed compost.

GERMINATION
Up to 14 days, sometimes longer.

TIME TILL FLOWERING
3–5 years.

ULTIMATE SIZE
10m x 10m (33ft x 33ft); prune
with care to keep within bounds.

These evergreen climbers are grown mainly
for their intriguing flowers, which are
produced over a long period from summer
to late autumn. The fruits are also beautiful.
They are all edible but only those of the
tender *Passiflora edulis* are actually worth
eating. This plant often seeds itself in gardens.

why grow from seed
Passiflora stems are soft and do not always provide good material
for cuttings. Seed is a good method of raising sturdy new plants.

aftercare
Pot the seedlings on in a soil-based compost (John Innes No.3)
and gradually acclimatise them to conditions outside the
propagator. Water them well and feed with a liquid fertiliser
while in active growth from spring to summer. Support the stems
with canes as they grow. Overwinter the seedlings in a cold frame.
Plant out, preferably in spring, when two or three years old.

FAR RIGHT *Passiflora fruits*
ripen to a warm orange
in autumn. Autumn
flowers can develop as
fruits, but these are
unlikely to ripen.

1 When the fruits have
ripened from green to
orange and are soft to the
touch, carefully cut them
from the plant. Cut each
fruit in half to expose the
seeds, which are held in a
gelatinous mass.

2 Wash the seeds then
dry them on absorbent
kitchen paper. Store them over
winter. The following spring
sow them in pots or trays of
standard seed compost, then
place them in a propagator at
21°C (70°F) until they germinate.

Pinus

Pine Pinaceae

WHEN TO SOW
Early spring, after stratification.

PRE-TREATMENT
Stratify the seed prior to sowing.

HOW TO SOW
Sow in pots or trays of standard seed compost.

GERMINATION
1–3 months.

TIME TILL FLOWERING
5 years.

ULTIMATE SIZE
20m x 9m (70ft x 29ft) but seed-raised plants can vary in size significantly, some being much more compact.

The pines are beautiful, many developing an impressive habit as they mature and all having that resinous scent that is so redolent of Mediterranean summers. Apart from gigantic species such as the Scot's pine (*Pinus sylvestris*), there are several that make appealing mounds no more than 1m (3ft) across.

why grow from seed
Pinus is a large genus, with some species being highly variable, so growing from seed is always exciting – you can never be entirely sure what the result will be.

aftercare
Sow the seeds in pots or trays of seed compost and keep outdoors until they germinate. Pot on the seedlings and feed them with a slow-release fertiliser in spring. Water them well when in active growth from spring to summer. Keep the seedlings in a cold frame over winter until they are large enough to plant out in their final positions.

FAR RIGHT *Pine cones open as they ripen to release the seeds.*

1 Remove the cones in autumn by twisting them from the branches. Place cones that are tightly closed near a heat source such as a radiator to encourage them to open. Tap the cones on a hard surface to release the winged seeds.

2 Remove the papery wings. Mix the seeds with perlite or vermiculite and seal in a plastic bag to stratify. Keep them at 4°C (39°F), or lower (for example in the freezer), for up to 12 weeks prior to sowing.

Prunus

Ornamental cherry Rosaceae

Prunus is a vast genus of trees and shrubs,
including both evergreen and deciduous
species as well as many plants grown for
their edible fruits – almonds, peaches, plums,
cherries – and ornamental versions. All have
delightful white spring flowers.

why grow from seed
Collect seed from plants if you are unable to find suitable
material for cuttings.

aftercare
Once you have sown the seeds, place the containers in a cold
frame. Pot on the seedlings as they appear, using soil-based
compost (John Innes No.3). Feed with a liquid fertiliser and water
the seedlings regularly while in active growth between spring
and summer. Overwinter the seedlings in a cold frame. Deciduous
species will drop their leaves in winter. Plant out when two years
old or more.

FAR RIGHT *Though they
might look like berries,*
prunus *fruits are drupes.*

1 In autumn when the
fruits are ripe, and
preferably after the first
frosts have occurred,
remove them from the
plant. Squash the fruits to
release the seeds. Each
fruit contains one seed.

2 Wash the seed in water,
then dry on absorbent
kitchen paper. Mix with
moistened perlite or
vermiculite in a plastic bag,
then place in the fridge for
four to six weeks. Sow the
seeds in pots or trays, then
cover with a layer of grit.

Pterocarya

Wing nut Juglandaceae

WHEN TO SOW
Autumn, when fresh.

PRE-TREATMENT
Stratify before sowing.

HOW TO SOW
In pots or trays of standard seed
compost topped with grit.

GERMINATION
8–12 weeks.

TIME TILL FLOWERING
5 years.

ULTIMATE SIZE
25m x 20m (80ft x 70ft), more or
less, depending on the species.

Wing nuts are stately trees with pendent
racemes of greenish flowers in late spring,
followed by intriguing chains of 'wooden'
seed cases in late summer/autumn. They
make excellent specimens, if ultimately
rather large.

why grow from seed

Seed is the most successful method of reproducing this tree –
the alternative being suckers, which are seldom produced in
great quantities.

aftercare

Once the seed has germinated, pot on the seedlings in soil-based
compost (John Innes No.3). Water the seedlings and feed with a
liquid fertiliser when they are in full growth from spring to
summer. Keep them in a cold frame over winter, when they will
be leafless.

FAR RIGHT *Pterocarya*
flowers, and the winged
seeds that follow, are
held in distinctive
hanging racemes.

1 Cut racemes of seeds
from the tree when
ripe from summer to
autumn. Pull the
individual seed cases
from the raceme.

2 Mix the seeds with
moistened perlite of
vermiculite and place in the
fridge for four weeks before
sowing. Sow the seeds in pots
or trays, top with horticultural
grit and place these outdoors.

Quercus

Oak Fagaceae

WHEN TO SOW
In autumn, when fresh.

PRE-TREATMENT
Scarify the seed prior to sowing.

HOW TO SOW
In tall pots filled with standard seed compost.

GERMINATION
3–6 months.

TIME TILL FLOWERING
5 years.

ULTIMATE SIZE
To 30m x 20m (100ft x 70ft), more or less, depending on the species.

Oaks are such magnificent trees it seems almost incredible that they grow from mere acorns. But they do, so it is always worth gathering a few and trying your hand before the squirrels get to them. Many oaks are deciduous, but there is also a handsome evergreen, *Quercus ilex*.

why grow from seed

Growing from seed is one of the most reliable methods of increasing stocks of this tree. Once germinated, the seedlings develop rapidly.

aftercare

Pot the seedlings on as they grow, in deep pots that will accommodate the long tap roots, using soil-based compost (John Innes No.3). Water and feed with a liquid fertiliser regularly when in active growth. Keep the containers in a cold frame over winter, when the seedlings will shed their leaves. Plant out when two years old or more.

FAR RIGHT *Acorns are large, nut-like seeds that are held in cups.*

1 Gently pull the seeds from the cups, which can then be discarded. Nick the coat of each seed with a sharp knife to speed up germination. Take care not to damage the tissue inside as you do this.

2 Plant the seeds in pots, or, preferably, long toms filled with standard seed compost. Place these outdoors. Oak seedlings rapidly develop long taproots.

Rosa glauca

syn. *R. rubrifolia* Rose Rosaceae

WHEN TO SOW
From late autumn onwards,
following stratification.

PRE-TREATMENT
Stratify the seed in the fridge
before sowing.

HOW TO SOW
In pots or trays of standard
seed compost topped with
horticultural grit or sharp sand.

GERMINATION
6 weeks to 2 years.

TIME TILL FLOWERING
2–4 years.

ULTIMATE SIZE
2m x 1.5m (6½ft x 5ft).

Most gardeners are surprised to learn that roses can be grown from seed, but please don't bother with trying to extract seed from hips that have formed on your glamorous hybrids. Only the species are worth trying. *R. glauca* has attractive pewter grey leaves and warm pink flowers in early summer that are followed by sealing wax red fruits.

why grow from seed

Seed is not much used for roses, but is a very reliable method for producing healthy plants of the species. Germination can be erratic, so keep faith and don't discard pots that show no sign of activity.

aftercare

Pot the seedlings on in soil-based compost (John Innes No.3). Water them when in active growth from spring to summer and feed with a liquid fertiliser. Keep young seedlings in a cold frame over winter, when they will lose their leaves. They can be planted out when two years old or more.

FAR RIGHT *The fruits, or hips, of* Rosa glauca *are bright shiny red when ripe.*

1 Squash the hips to release the seeds. Wash these in water, then dry them on absorbent kitchen paper. Mix with perlite or vermiculite.

2 Stratify the seeds for three to six weeks in the fridge before sowing. Once germinated, the seedlings will develop rapidly and in two years the plant will really look like a rose.

Sorbus

Rowan Rosaceae

WHEN TO SOW
When ripe in autumn.

PRE-TREATMENT
Stratify the seed before sowing.

HOW TO SOW
In pots or trays of standard seed compost, topped with grit or sharp sand.

GERMINATION
1–4 weeks.

TIME TILL FLOWERING
3–5 years.

ULTIMATE SIZE
8m x 6m (26ft x 20ft) more or less, depending on the species.

The rowans are some of the most recommendable garden trees. Light and airy in habit – hence they do not cast that leaden shade in summer – they have at least two seasons of interest. Clusters of white spring flowers are followed by impressive white, pink, yellow or red autumn berries. If you want to collect seed, be sure to collect the berries before the birds get to them. They are usually stripped within a matter of weeks.

why grow from seed
Most of the rowans grown in gardens are species, so it is well worth raising new stocks from seed.

aftercare
Pot the seedlings on in soil-based compost (John Innes No.3). Feed with a general fertiliser when in active growth from spring to summer and keep them well watered. Put young seedlings in a cold frame over winter, when they will lose their leaves. Plant the seedlings out when they are large enough.

FAR RIGHT *Sorbus fruits ripen in autumn as the leaves turn colour and are shed.*

1 Cut the berries from the tree in mid- to late autumn, preferably after a frost has softened them. Squash the berries to release the seeds. Wash the seeds and dry them on absorbent kitchen paper.

2 Mix with moistened perlite or vermiculite and put in a clear plastic bag. Keep the seeds in the fridge for six to eight weeks, then sow in pots or trays of seed compost topped with grit or sharp sand. Keep the containers at 15°C (59°F) until the seed has germinated.

Taxus baccata

Yew Taxaceae

WHEN TO SOW
Autumn.

PRE-TREATMENT
Stratify the seed in the fridge or freezer before sowing.

HOW TO SOW
In pots or trays of standard seed compost topped with grit or sharp sand.

GERMINATION
Usually within 6 to 12 months.

TIME TILL FLOWERING
3–5 years.

ULTIMATE SIZE
10–20m x 8–10m (33–70ft x 26–33ft) as a freestanding tree, though habits can vary – some seedlings being more compact.

A number one choice for hedging and topiary – and for specimens, given a century or two – yew is as easily raised from seed as from cuttings. Seedlings vary – some will be a sinister, almost blackish green, while others will gleam like old gold. Technically, the berries are cones. Examine one, and you will see that it is open at one end. A true berry is closed.

why grow from seed
While you can grow this plant from cuttings, seed gives rather less predictable results, which – if you are intending to create a hedge – can prove attractive in the end.

aftercare
Pot up the seedlings in containers filled with a soil-based compost (John Innes No.3). Pot them on annually until they are large enough to plant out in their final positions, or grow on in a nursery bed. While they are in containers, water them well during the growing season and feed at the start of the season with a slow-release fertiliser.

FAR RIGHT *Coral red yew berries stud the trees during autumn.*

1 Squash the berries to release the seeds. Each fruit contains a single seed. Wash the seeds, then dry them on absorbent kitchen paper.

2 Mix the seeds with perlite or vermiculite in a plastic bag, then place in the fridge or freezer for six to eight weeks before sowing in standard seed compost. Top with grit or sharp sand.

Viburnum tinus

Laurustinus Caprifoliaceae

WHEN TO SOW
Autumn.

PRE-TREATMENT
Stratify the seed in the fridge before sowing.

HOW TO SOW
In pots or trays of standard seed compost topped with grit or sharp sand.

GERMINATION
Up to 6 months or more; germination can be erratic.

TIME TILL FLOWERING
3 years.

ULTIMATE SIZE
3m x 3m (10ft x 10ft), though seedlings can be more compact.

An essential plant for the winter garden, this reliable evergreen starts pushing out its clusters of white flowers in late autumn, carrying on throughout the winter and well into the following spring. By the time the metallic blue berries are ripening in autumn, the next crop of flowers is already opening.

why grow from seed
Though this species shows great genetic stability, variation in seedlings is possible – some being more free-flowering or compact than others.

aftercare
Sow the seed in pots or trays of seed compost, top with grit or sharp sand, then place outdoors. Pot up the seedlings, using soil-based compost (John Innes No.3). Water the plants regularly while in full growth in spring and summer and feed with a liquid fertiliser. Keep the seedlings in a cold frame over winter, and water them periodically to prevent leaf drop. Plant them out when large enough, usually when they are two years old or more.

FAR RIGHT *Viburnum* tinus *fruits are a metallic blackish blue when ripe.*

1 Remove ripe fruits from the stems in mid- to late autumn, ideally after a frost has softened them. Each berry contains one seed.

2 The berries are not fleshy, so it is easiest to extract the seed by scraping the seed coat away with a small, sharp knife. Mix the seed with moistened perlite or vermiculite, seal in a plastic bag, then keep in the fridge for up to six weeks.

perennials and bulbs

Acanthus

Bear's breeches Acanthaceae

WHEN TO SOW
Spring or autumn.

PRE-TREATMENT
None necessary.

HOW TO SOW
In pots or trays of standard seed compost outdoors.

GERMINATION
Usually around 14 days, longer at low temperatures; autumn sowings may not germinate until the following spring.

TIME TILL FLOWERING
3 years.

ULTIMATE SIZE
1.2m x 1m (4ft x 3ft).

These stately perennials have large, glossy leaves that die back in winter and sinister-looking spikes of hooded flowers in early summer. Take care when you cut down the flowered stems. The bracts surrounding the seeds have very sharp spikes.

why grow from seed
This perennial is rather unusual in that only species are grown and there are no named varieties. Such is the genetic stability that you know exactly what you'll be getting when you grow from seed.

aftercare
You can speed up germination by keeping the seeds at 18°C (64°F) in a propagator. Pot the seedlings on in soil-based compost (John Innes No.2) as they grow, water them and feed with a general fertiliser. Plants die back in autumn. Year-old seedlings can be lined out in a nursery bed. Protect them over winter with a cloche. Overwinter young plants grown in pots in a cold frame.

FAR RIGHT *The bracts turn papery and the fruits ripen to blackish brown in mid- to late autumn.*

1 Cut down the flowered stems in late summer to early autumn, when the fruits darken and the surrounding bracts dry out and become papery. Carefully pull the fruits from the bracts.

2 Gently squash the fruits between finger and thumb to release the seeds. Wash them if they do not emerge cleanly and dry before sowing. Sow in pots or trays of standard seed compost.

Agapanthus

African blue lily Alliaceae/Liliaceae

WHEN TO SOW
Spring or autumn.

PRE-TREATMENT
None necessary.

HOW TO SOW
In pots or trays of standard seed compost with added grit, perlite or vermiculite.

GERMINATION
18–24 days.

TIME TILL FLOWERING
2–3 years.

ULTIMATE SIZE
90cm x 60cm (36in x 24in).

Few plants can match the blue of agapanthus, a perennial that produces its flowers in rounded heads in late summer to autumn. There are also white forms, but somehow these seem less desirable. They thrive in containers – indeed, they seem to flower most freely when they have become congested after a number of years.

why grow from seed

Plants flower best where left undisturbed. Rather than splitting them, collect seed. New plants are easily raised from seed, and seedlings show some variation in the depth of blue of the flowers – an enticing prospect.

aftercare

Pot on the seedlings as they grow, using a soil-based compost (John Innes No.2) with added grit, perlite or vermiculite. Water and feed regularly when in full growth in spring and summer. Keep seedlings in a cold frame over winter until they reach flowering size.

FAR RIGHT *Agapanthus seeds usually do not ripen until mid- to late autumn.*

1 Cut the flowered stems from the plant in autumn. If the seed cases are still green and are yet to split open, hang them upside down to dry. As they ripen, individual cases split lengthways to release several black seeds.

2 Remove the seeds from their cases and clean off any papery matter adhering to them. Either sow immediately or store the seed over winter ready for sowing the following spring.

Alcea

Hollyhock Malvaceae

WHEN TO SOW
Late summer to autumn;
bought seed can be sown
in spring.

PRE-TREATMENT
None necessary.

HOW TO SOW
In pots or trays of standard seed
compost topped with sharp
sand, perlite or vermiculite.

GERMINATION
6–10 days at 18°C (64°F); autumn
sowings may take longer.

TIME TILL FLOWERING
1 year; early sowings can flower
the same year.

ULTIMATE SIZE
1.5–2.5m x 60cm (5–8ft x 24in).

These are real cottage garden perennials,
with tall, stately spires of mallow flowers in
summer in white or soft shades of cream
and pink – plus a very dramatic reddish
purple. The double forms are also desirable.

why grow from seed

All hollyhocks are susceptible to rust, so it is a good idea to
replace your stocks periodically with fresh plants raised from
seed. Many gardeners treat them as annuals or biennials, and
you will come across various strains in seed catalogues and
at garden centres. Seed you collect yourself will yield less
predictable results.

aftercare

Pot the seedlings on individually using soil-based compost
(John Innes No.2) or line out in a nursery bed until large enough
to plant out, usually after one year. Early sowings can flower
the same year. Water and feed plants in pots regularly in spring
and summer.

FAR RIGHT *Hollyhock*
seedheads ripen
usually from late
summer onwards.

1 Cut the stems from
the plant as they dry
out. The seed cases should
be starting to open. Shake
them gently to release the
comma-shaped seeds.
Either sow immediately or
store over winter for
sowing in spring.

2 Sow the seeds in pots or
trays of standard seed
compost. Lightly press them
into the compost surface,
then top with sharp sand,
perlite or vermiculite.

Allium

Ornamental onion Liliaceae

The heads of the alliums are of geometric
precision, perfect globes of flowers in white,
mauve, yellow and metallic blue-purple.
Some species flower in mid-spring, others
in early summer. Seed ripens around eight
to twelve weeks after flowering.

why grow from seed
The bulbs of several of the larger species can be costly, so it is well
worth collecting seed when you can – provided you can bear the
wait till the seedlings flower.

aftercare
Water the seedlings as they grow and feed with a general
fertiliser. Stop watering and feeding when the topgrowth starts
to die back in late summer to autumn. Pot the bulblets on
annually in autumn, using soil-based compost (John Innes No.2)
with added grit, sand, perlite or vermiculite, until large enough
to plant out.

FAR RIGHT *Allium
seedheads have a
geometric perfection.*

1 Detach individual seed
cases as they dry and
split open and then shake
them gently to release
the seeds. Sow the seeds
in pots or trays filled with
a gritty compost and
place outdoors.

2 In the autumn after the
seeds have germinated,
when the topgrowth has died
back, knock out the pots and
separate out the bulblets. Pot
these up in fresh compost for
growing on the following year.

Alstroemeria

Peruvian lily Alstroemeriaceae

WHEN TO SOW
In late summer to autumn, when ripe.

PRE-TREATMENT
None necessary.

HOW TO SOW
In pots of soil-based compost (John Innes No.2) topped with grit, perlite or vermiculite.

GERMINATION
10–12 weeks or longer; germination can be erratic.

TIME TILL FLOWERING
2–3 years.

ULTIMATE SIZE
60cm x 60cm (24in x 24in).

These lovely plants produce their exquisitely marked flowers in summer. In cold areas, be sure to give them a warm, sheltered spot and leave them undisturbed. After a few years they will develop into sizeable clumps.

why grow from seed
Peruvian lilies are virtually impossible to transplant, as the roots are so brittle. So if you want to increase your stocks it is best to raise new plants from seed in pots for planting out once they reach flowering size.

aftercare
Keep the sown seed at 20°C (68°F) for three weeks, then transfer to the refrigerator for four weeks. After this, keep the seed at 20°C (68°F) for around four weeks or until the seed germinates. Feed with a general fertiliser and water well when the seedlings are in full growth. They will die back completely each autumn.

FAR RIGHT *Peruvian lily seedheads are inflated and almost woody as they dry out.*

1 Cut the flowered stems from the plant when they are dry in mid- to late autumn. Split the seed cases with care, as they are rather brittle. Tap out the spherical, black seeds.

2 Sow the seeds in pots filled with soil-based compost (John Innes No.2). Peruvian lilies resent disturbance, so use a pot that will accommodate the fully grown plant. Top with grit, perlite or vermiculite.

Eucomis bicolor

Pineapple flower, pineapple lily Hyacinthaceae/Liliaceae

WHEN TO SOW
Spring.

PRE-TREATMENT
None necessary.

HOW TO SOW
Sow in pots or trays of standard seed compost with added grit, perlite or vermiculite.

GERMINATION
18–24 days.

TIME TILL FLOWERING
2–3 years.

ULTIMATE SIZE
30–60cm x 20cm
(12–24in x 8in).

This South African bulb produces an upright spike of flowers that looks just like a pineapple. It is not a reliably hardy plant, but makes an ideal choice for a container that can be brought under cover over winter in cold areas.

why grow from seed
This bulb is of borderline hardiness, so is prone to frost damage. Growing new plants from seed is the best method of maintaining healthy stocks of potential replacements.

aftercare
Keep the seed at 20°C (68°F) until germinated. Feed with a general fertiliser and water the seedlings well when in full growth. Topgrowth dies back completely each autumn. Pot on the bulblets annually in spring or autumn until they reach flowering size, using a soil-based compost (John Innes No.2) with added grit, perlite or vermiculite.

FAR RIGHT *Eucomis seedheads are almost as attractive as the flowers.*

1 Cut the flowered stems from the plant when the seed cases dry out. As they split open the black seeds within are clearly revealed.

2 Gently pick the seeds from the papery cases, with a finger and thumb if you are dexterous. Alternatively, a pair of tweezers can help. Sow in pots or trays filled with a free-draining compost.

FERNS

Pteridophyta

WHEN TO SOW
Summer to autumn, when the spores are ripe.

PRE-TREATMENT
None necessary.

HOW TO SOW
In pots or trays of standard seed compost. Water the compost with boiling water to sterilise it before sowing.

GERMINATION
4–6 weeks.

ULTIMATE SIZE
23cm x 23cm (9in x 9in) to 2m x 2m (6½ft x 6½ft), depending on the species.

Ferns, some evergreen, some deciduous, are ideal plants for shade, particularly if the soil is damp. They are primitive plants that do not flower and set seed as such – reproduction occurs by means of spores.

why grow from spores

Not all ferns divide easily, so growing from spores is the best way of raising new plants in quantity. In some species, astonishing variations can occur, with a high degree of crimping and curling of the fronds.

aftercare

After a few days, carefully lift the frond from the paper. The spores left behind leave a ghostly image. Prepare pots or trays of seed compost. Tap the spores onto the compost surface, then place in a propagator in a warm place out of direct sunlight. Within a few weeks, a green film should appear on the surface. When little fronds appear, pot them on into trays or modules. Pot up the little ferns individually into soil-based compost (John Innes No.2) when large enough. At no time of their development should the developing ferns be allowed to dry out. Feed the young plants when they are in growth with a general fertiliser.

FAR RIGHT *Place a frond on a sheet of paper to trap the spores.*

1 From summer to autumn look for mature fronds on the plant. Cut each one at the base with scissors or secateurs.

2 Turn each frond over and look for signs of blistering on the underside, indicating that the spores are ripe. Place the frond on a sheet of paper and wait for the spores to be released.

GRASSES

Gramineae and Poaceae

WHEN TO SOW
Preferably in autumn, as soon as the seed is ripe, or spring.

PRE-TREATMENT
None necessary.

HOW TO SOW
Sow in pots or trays of standard seed compost topped with horticultural grit or sharp sand.

GERMINATION
2 weeks, or longer, depending on the species.

TIME TILL FLOWERING
2–4 years.

ULTIMATE SIZE
15cm x 15cm (6in x 6in) to 1.5m x 1.5m (5ft x 5ft), depending on the species.

Grasses comprise a huge group of plants, evergreens and deciduous species and even some annuals. There really is a grass for every situation – sun, shade, damp ground, dry ground – so choose your varieties with care. Species can all be raised easily from seed.

why grow from seed

It is always rewarding to grow grasses from seed, as exciting forms can occur. Some grasses are annuals that can only be raised from seed. They are nearly all grown for their long-lasting flowers and seedheads that stay on the plant often well into winter. This means there is always a good supply of seeds available.

aftercare

Place the pots outdoors or in a cold frame until germinated. Keep the seedlings in a cold frame over winter. Remember that seedlings of deciduous species will die right back. Pot the seedlings on the following spring in soil-based compost (John Innes No.2). Feed with a general fertiliser and water them well while in full growth from spring to autumn.

FAR RIGHT *Perennial grass seedlings should be large enough to plant out a few months after sowing.*

1 Cut the seedheads from the plant in late summer to autumn when they are dry and beige-brown in colour. Gently pull the seeds from the stems. (They can be sticky.)

2 Surface sow the seeds in pots or trays of seed compost. Lightly cover with horticultural grit or sharp sand to hold the seeds in place. Seed can also be stored over winter for spring sowing, but a smaller percentage will germinate.

Helleborus

Hellebore Ranunculaceae

WHEN TO SOW
Summer to autumn when the seed is ripe; seed can also be stored over winter and sown in spring.

PRE-TREATMENT
None necessary.

HOW TO SOW
Sow in pots or trays of standard seed compost topped with grit.

GERMINATION
Sometimes around 4 weeks; seed sown late in the year may not germinate until the following spring. Germination can be erratic, sometimes taking up to 12 months.

TIME TILL FLOWERING
2 years.

ULTIMATE SIZE
45cm x 45cm (18in x 18in), more or less, depending on the species.

These worthwhile evergreens are increasingly popular. Their cup-shaped flowers, sometimes dramatically coloured, open from mid-winter until well into spring. An increasing number of hybrids are appearing in commerce, but they in no way outclass the species – all of which can be grown from seed.

why grow from seed

Many hellebores can take a season or two to recover from division, so it is often a better bet to raise new plants from seed to increase stocks. *H. orientalis* in particular has a big gene pool, and excitingly coloured seedlings are always a possibility.

aftercare

Once germinated, grow on the seedlings in individual pots, using soil-based compost (John Innes No.2). Feed with a general fertiliser and water well when in full growth from spring to summer. Plant them in their final positions when they reach flowering size. Keep transplants well watered – they can be slow to establish.

FAR RIGHT *Make sure transplants don't dry out by wrapping in dampened newspaper.*

1 Collect the seed as the seed cases ripen and split open, usually around 12 weeks after the flowers have opened.

2 Surface sow the seed in pots or trays, then top with horticultural grit. Place the containers outdoors to break the seeds' dormancy.

Iris foetidissima

Stinking gladwyn, stinking iris Iridaceae

WHEN TO SOW
Autumn, as soon as the seeds
are ripe.

PRE-TREATMENT
None necessary.

HOW TO SOW
Sow the seeds in pots or trays
of standard seed compost,
top with horticultural grit and
place outdoors.

GERMINATION
4–12 months.

TIME TILL FLOWERING
2 years.

ULTIMATE SIZE
90cm x 15cm (36in x 6in).

Please don't let this plant's common name
put you off, or the fact that it is often defined
as a bog plant. All the smelly parts are
underground. The plant is grown less for its
dull purple flowers, which are small in
relation to the overall size of the plant, than
the brilliant orange seeds – these are real
eyecatchers in the winter garden.

why grow from seed

If you have only a single specimen of this plant and want to
reproduce it in quantity, seed is the quickest way of building
up numbers.

aftercare

Surface sow the seed, then top with a layer of horticultural grit.
Place the containers outdoors. Once germinated, water and feed
the seedlings regularly while they are in active growth. These are
moisture-loving plants, so make sure the seedlings never dry out.
Overwinter the seedlings in a cold frame. Plant out in their final
positions when large enough, usually after one or two years.

FAR RIGHT *Seed cases split
open in late autumn to
reveal fleshy, bright
orange fruits.*

1 Carefully remove the
berries from the seed
cases as these split in mid-
to late autumn. Lightly
squash them to release
the seeds.

2 Wash the seeds in water
and dry on absorbent
kitchen paper. Iris seed is best
sown immediately, but can be
stored over winter for sowing
the following spring.

Liatris spicata

syn. *L. callilepis of gardens* Gayfeather Asteraceae/Compositae

WHEN TO SOW
Autumn or spring; autumn sowings may not germinate until the following spring.

PRE-TREATMENT
None necessary.

HOW TO SOW
In pots or trays of standard seed compost topped with fine grit or sharp sand.

GERMINATION
3–4 weeks; germination can be quicker at 18°C (64°F).

TIME TILL FLOWERING
2 years.

ULTIMATE SIZE
1.5m x 45cm (5ft x 18in).

A curious plant – not vivid enough to be described as architectural or bold enough in colour to take centre stage – its muted mauve flower spikes add depth to late summer borders. It belongs to the daisy tribe, though it looks nothing like a daisy – so it makes a good contrast to late-flowering asters and rudbeckias.

why grow from seed

Since the species is such a handsome plant, it is always worth growing it from seed. Seedlings can show some variation in flower colour. Dark purple and white forms may appear.

aftercare

Place the pots in a propagator or cold frame until the seeds have germinated. Pot up the seedlings in soil-based compost (John Innes No.2) and feed and water well when in active growth from spring to summer. They will die back each autumn. Plant out the seedlings when large enough, usually after one or two years.

FAR RIGHT *Liatris seed heads are like bottlebrushes, and the seeds are dispersed on the wind.*

1 In mid- to late autumn, as the seedheads dry out and turn fluffy, cut the flowered stems from the plant. Pick off the seeds from the flower spike.

2 Sow the seed on the surface of pots or trays filled with standard seed compost. Topping them with a layer of fine grit or sharp sand will help hold them firmly in place.

Lilium regale

Regal lily Liliaceae

WHEN TO SOW
In autumn, as the seed cases split open. Seed can also be stored for sowing in spring.

PRE-TREATMENT
None necessary.

HOW TO SOW
In pots or trays of standard seed compost topped with horticultural grit or sharp sand.

GERMINATION
2–4 weeks; autumn sowings may not germinate until the following spring.

TIME TILL FLOWERING
3 years.

ULTIMATE SIZE
60cm or more x 10cm (2ft x 4in).

Is this not the most beautiful of all lilies? You are bound to agree when the richly scented white trumpets open in summer. Seed-raised plants vary in the degree of purple staining on the outsides of the flowers. Some will be richly marked, while others will be virtually pure white.

why grow from seed
Raising lilies from seed is a guaranteed method of producing virus-free stock. In borders, especially if the ground becomes over-moist, bulbs can die off underground, so this is the best method of keeping up numbers.

aftercare
Feed the seedlings when they are in active growth in spring and summer with a general-purpose fertiliser. Each autumn, when the topgrowth has died down, knock out the bulblets from the pots and pot them up into fresh compost (John Innes No.2), with added grit, perlite or vermiculite, always burying them to twice their own depth. Keep them in a cold frame over winter.

FAR RIGHT *Lily seedheads turn light brown and split lengthways as they ripen to release the copious seeds.*

1 Gently shake the open seed cases to release the seeds – they are light and flat, but easy enough to handle individually. Surface sow the seeds in pots or trays and top with a light layer of horticultural grit or sharp sand.

2 Place the pots outdoors. Overwinter them in a cold frame. Keep potting on the bulblets annually each autumn. (A bulblet looks like a miniature version of a mature bulb.)

Lupinus

Lupin Leguminosae/Papilionaceae

WHEN TO SOW
Sow in spring or autumn.

PRE-TREATMENT
Nick the seed, rub with
sandpaper or soak for 24 hours
before sowing.

HOW TO SOW
Sow in pots, trays or modules of
standard seed compost topped
with horticultural grit, sharp
sand, perlite or vermiculite.

GERMINATION
2–3 weeks.

TIME TILL FLOWERING
2 years.

ULTIMATE SIZE
1m x 75cm (3ft x 30in).

For solid spires of rich colour in the
border, lupins are ideal. Less elegant than
delphiniums, they nevertheless provide a
wider colour range: white, cream, pink, red,
purple and blue. They seem to do best on
acid soil.

why grow from seed

Lupins are susceptible to certain diseases and viruses. For the
general health of the garden, replace older, more vulnerable
plants with fresh, seed-raised plants. You can collect seed from
your own plants or buy the seed of certain strains.

aftercare

Pot on the seedlings as they grow. Overwinter them in a cold
frame. Feed with a general-purpose fertiliser and water them
regularly when they are in active growth from spring to summer.
Plant them out in their final positions when they reach flowering
size, usually after a year.

FAR RIGHT *Lupin seed
cases are like furry bean
pods. A single plant
usually produces
quantities of seeds.*

1 Cut flowered stems
from the plant in mid-
to late autumn. Carefully
split individual seed cases
in order to release the
round, black seeds.

2 Soak the seeds in warm
water for 24 hours to
accelerate germination.
Then sow in pots, trays or
modules filled with standard
seed compost. Top with
horticultural grit, sharp sand,
perlite or vermiculite.

Nectaroscordum siculum

syn. *Allium siculum* Alliaceae/Liliaceae

WHEN TO SOW
Autumn or spring; autumn sowings may not germinate until the following spring.

PRE-TREATMENT
None necessary.

HOW TO SOW
Sow in pots or trays of standard seed compost topped with horticultural grit or sharp sand.

GERMINATION
2–4 weeks, autumn sowings sometimes take longer.

TIME TILL FLOWERING
3 years.

ULTIMATE SIZE
1.2m x 10cm (4ft x 4in).

This plant is a real favourite of mine, though its appeal may not be immediately obvious. The bell-like flowers, in shades of green and cream, hang down on short stems in a modest, understated way. Try planting it with roses for a contrast in form.

why grow from seed
To save digging up bulbs – a risky process, as it is easy to damage them – grow from seed. A single plant produces copious amounts and they germinate readily.

aftercare
Place the pots outdoors until the seed has germinated. Feed with a general-purpose fertiliser and water the seedlings well when in active growth from spring to summer. After the topgrowth has died down in autumn, knock out the compost and excavate the bulblets. Pot them on in fresh soil-based compost (John Innes No.2) with added grit and keep them in a cold frame over winter.

FAR RIGHT *As this plant's seedheads dry out they start to split to release the seeds.*

1 Cut the stems from the plant in late summer to autumn when the seed cases are starting to split. Gently shake the seeds free, then surface sow them. Top with a light layer of horticultural grit or sharp sand.

2 In autumn, when the topgrowth has died down, shake out the contents and clean off individual bulblets. Pot these on annually until they reach flowering size. Always bury the bulblets to twice their own depth.

Paeonia mlokosewitschii

Caucasian peony Paeoniaceae

WHEN TO SOW
Autumn, when ripe; seed can also be stored for sowing in spring.

PRE-TREATMENT
Stratify the seed in the fridge or outdoors.

HOW TO SOW
Sow in pots or trays of soil-based compost (John Innes No.2).

GERMINATION
6–18 months; germination can be erratic.

TIME TILL FLOWERING
3–4 years.

ULTIMATE SIZE
60cm x 60cm (24in x 24in).

This beautiful plant is often called 'Molly the witch', a simple English version of its unpronounceable botanical name. It remains one of the most desirable of all perennials, though its moonlit yellow flowers sit like chalices among the pewter grey leaves for no longer than a week in spring. A truly charismatic plant.

why grow from seed

With their fleshy, easily damaged roots, peonies usually take some years to recover if transplanted. Such is the rarity of this plant that new plants should be grown from seed as often as possible.

aftercare

Either stratify the seed artificially as described below, or sow the seed fresh and keep the pots outdoors. Exposure to frost is necessary to break the seeds' dormancy, so protection in a cold frame is not necessary. Seed may not germinate until it has experienced two periods of cold over successive winters. Feed seedlings with a general fertiliser when in active growth and overwinter in a cold frame until large enough to plant out, usually after two or three years.

FAR RIGHT *The seeds of this plant are held in distinctive cases lined with red.*

1 Remove the seed cases from the plant in mid- to late summer, as they dry out and split to reveal their seeds. Mix the seed with dampened perlite or vermiculite.

2 Keep the seed for three to four weeks in the fridge, then sow in pots of soil-based compost (John Innes No.2) and place outdoors. Pot the seedlings on as they grow, taking great care not to damage the thick but rather brittle roots.

Papaver orientale

Oriental poppy Papaveraceae

WHEN TO SOW
Late summer, when fresh,
or spring.

PRE-TREATMENT
None necessary.

HOW TO SOW
In pots or trays of standard
seed compost.

GERMINATION
Usually within 2 weeks (spring
sowings); late summer sowings
may not germinate until the
following spring.

TIME TILL FLOWERING
2 years.

ULTIMATE SIZE
90cm x 90cm (36in x 36in).

Poppies delight in late spring with their satin-textured flowers dramatically marked with black within. Flowers of seed-raised plants are usually gleaming red, though shades of pink – and doubles – also occur.

why grow from seed

Growing from seed is the quickest way of building up stocks of poppies, as the plants do not divide readily.

aftercare

Pot on the seedlings annually, using a soil-based compost (John Innes No.2), or transfer them to a nursery bed. Feed seedlings in containers with a general fertiliser during spring and summer and water them regularly. The topgrowth dies back in winter. Plant the young poppies out in their final positions when they reach flowering size.

FAR RIGHT *Poppy seedheads are like pepper pots and rattle when the seed is ripe.*

1 From late summer onwards, cut dried stems from the plant. Tap the seedheads over a piece of paper to catch the seeds. Sow the seed in pots or trays and keep in a cold frame until they germinate. Seed can also be stored over winter and sown in spring.

2 Pot the seedlings on as they grow. Pot them up individually when large enough so they can be given room to develop. Plant them out in their flowering positions when large enough.

Phlomis russeliana

syn. *P. samia of gardens, P. viscosa of gardens* Labiatae/Lamiaceae

WHEN TO SOW
Autumn or spring; autumn
sowings may not germinate
until the following spring.

PRE-TREATMENT
None necessary.

HOW TO SOW
In pots or trays of standard
seed compost with added grit,
perlite or vermiculite.

GERMINATION
2–4 weeks.

TIME TILL FLOWERING
2 years.

ULTIMATE SIZE
90cm x 75cm (36in x 30in).

Perennial phlomis, with their large, soft
green leaves that hang from the stems and
whorls of hooded, soft yellow flowers, are
much less commonly grown than the
shrubby types. However, this species from
the Middle East makes a splendid foil to
other more dramatic perennials.

why grow from seed

This is one of those architectural plants that it's best not to cut
down after flowering – the stiff stems and whorled seed cases are
decorative when rimed with frost in winter. So why not collect
some seed in autumn? While mature plants can be divided, to
produce quantities of this plant quickly, seed is the best option.

aftercare

Pot the seedlings up individually into pots of soil-based compost
(John Innes No.2) or multi-purpose compost. Alternatively, line
out in a nursery bed. Water and feed with a general garden
fertiliser when in growth between spring and autumn. Protect
from frost in winter: place containers in a cold frame and cover
plants in the open ground with a cloche.

FAR RIGHT *Phlomis seeds
are held in cases spaced
at regular intervals up
the stem.*

1 Cut the stems from
the plant when they
have dried out and are
beige-brown in colour.
Gently shake the seeds
from the cases. Either sow
immediately or store over
winter for sowing the
following spring.

2 Sow the seed in pots or
trays of standard seed
compost with added grit,
perlite or vermiculite. To speed
up germination, place in a
propagator at 15–18°C
(59–64°F).

Verbena bonariensis

syn. *V. patagonica* Verbenacae

WHEN TO SOW
Autumn or spring to summer outdoors; sowings can also be made in a propagator from late winter.

PRE-TREATMENT
None necessary.

HOW TO SOW
Sow in pots or trays of standard seed compost topped with sharp sand, perlite or vermiculite.

GERMINATION
2–3 weeks.

TIME TILL FLOWERING
2 years, although early sowings can flower the same season.

ULTIMATE SIZE
1.5m x 30cm (5ft x 12in).

Nothing has been more remarkable than this plant's deserved rise in popularity over recent years. Carried on tall, thin stems that are square in cross-section, the flower heads are small, but their luminous violet makes quite an effect, especially where they are grown in quantity scattered among lower-growing plants. A psychedelic haze of purple seems to hover in the air like a dust cloud.

why grow from seed
You can hardly have enough of this plant, and growing from seed is the most economical way of achieving the best effect in the shortest amount of time. And it's only of borderline hardiness and short-lived, so you need to keep your stocks up.

aftercare
Pot the seedlings on as they grow into pots of soil-based compost (John Innes No.2). Feed and water the seedlings regularly while they are in active growth in spring and summer. Plant out in their flowering positions when large enough. Summer sowings should be overwintered in a cold frame.

FAR RIGHT *This young seedling, dug up in autumn, will flower next year.*

1 Either collect seed from the seed cases in late summer/autumn or buy packets of seed. The seeds are quite fine, but you should still be able to sow them individually.

2 Surface sow the seeds, then top with a thin layer of sharp sand, perlite or vermiculite. Keep at a temperature of 15–20°C (59–68°F) until germinated. Summer sowings can be germinated outdoors.

annuals and biennials

Dianthus barbatus

Sweet William Caryophyllaceae

WHEN TO SOW
Spring to autumn (but not during hot weather in summer); early spring sowings can flower the same year.

PRE-TREATMENT
None necessary.

HOW TO SOW
Sow in pots or trays of standard seed compost and top with perlite, vermiculite or grit.

GERMINATION
14–30 days.

TIME TILL FLOWERING
5–9 months, depending on the sowing time.

ULTIMATE SIZE
70cm x 30cm (28in x 12in), or less; some varieties are dwarf.

Everybody loves these hardy biennials, with their domed heads of white, pink or dusky red flowers. Most, though not all, are deliciously scented, so choose your varieties with care if you really want that distinctive powdery fragrance. Traditionally they are spring flowers, but some modern varieties can be treated as annuals and will flower throughout the summer.

why grow from seed
Dianthus barbatus is actually a short-lived hardy perennial, but you will get the best results by raising new plants from seed every year.

aftercare
Once germinated, grow the seedlings on at cooler temperatures. Pot up the seedlings using soil-based compost (John Innes No.2). Water and feed them with a liquid fertiliser regularly until large enough to plant out – when about 15cm (6in) tall. Autumn sowings made for early flowers the following year should be kept in a cold frame over winter.

FAR RIGHT *Seedlings will be large enough to plant out six to eight weeks after germinating.*

1 Tip out the seeds from the packet. They are just about large enough to handle individually. You can reserve some for later sowings.

2 Sow the seeds in pots, trays or modules, using standard seed compost. Top with perlite, vermiculite or grit. Cover with clear plastic or place in a propagator and keep at 15–20°C (59–68°F) until germinated.

Erysimum cheiri

syn. *Cheiranthus cheiri* Wallflower Brassicaceae/Cruciferae

WHEN TO SOW
Spring to late summer.

PRE-TREATMENT
None necessary.

HOW TO SOW
Sow in pots, trays or modules
that are filled with standard
seed compost topped with
horticultural grit, perlite or
vermiculite. Alternatively, sow
in seed beds outdoors.

GERMINATION
14–21 days.

TIME TILL FLOWERING
9–10 months.

ULTIMATE SIZE
30cm x 30cm (12in x 12in), more
or less, depending on the variety.

Wallflowers are classic spring-flowering
hardy biennials for use with tulips, for which
they are the perfect foil. Single-coloured
forms are available – cream, yellow and rich
carmine red – as well as mixtures. It's not a
good idea to grow wallflowers in the same
site every year. Like cabbages, to which they
are related, they are susceptible to club root,
a disease that can persist in the soil. If you
think you have a problem, grow them in
large containers with tulips.

why grow from seed
Though these plants can be perennial, for the best display they
should be replaced annually with fresh stock.

aftercare
Pot on seedlings raised in containers using soil-based compost
(John Innes No.2). Transfer spring sowings to their flowering
positions in autumn. Smaller plants raised from seed germinated
later in the season are best overwintered in a cold frame. If
sown in seed beds, protect with a cloche or horticultural fleece
during cold weather.

FAR RIGHT *Pot up seedlings
in containers when they
are large enough.*

1 Tip the seeds from
the packet. They are
fairly large, so you should
find that they are easy to
sow individually.

2 Sow a small number
in individual pots
or modules, or in rows
in trays, filled with standard
seed compost. Top with
grit, perlite or vermiculite.
Alternatively, sow the seeds
outdoors in drills.

Helianthus annus

Sunflower Asteraceae/Compositae

WHEN TO SOW
Sow in spring for flowers the same year. Autumn sowings can be overwintered for early flowers the following year.

PRE-TREATMENT
None necessary.

HOW TO SOW
Sow in pots of standard seed compost or in drills outdoors.

GERMINATION
7–21 days.

TIME TILL FLOWERING
3–4 months; autumn sowings 6–8 months.

ULTIMATE SIZE
2.5m x 60cm (8ft x 24in), or less; some varieties are dwarf.

Everyone loves sunflowers, hardy annuals that produce large cheery daisies in summer. Some varieties are giants that turn their disc-like flowers to the sun at the tops of tall, thick stems, but there are also more modest varieties that are excellent in borders and terrific for cutting. Colours include cream, yellow and a rich, almost blackish, red.

why grow from seed

Many people grow sunflowers just for the sake of the seeds – a valuable food source for birds in winter. If you think they can spare some, steal a few from the flower heads in late autumn. Remember that seed from named varieties will revert to the species.

aftercare

Pot on the seedlings as they grow, using soil-based compost (John Innes No.1 or No.2). Water and feed them with a liquid fertiliser regularly. Protect seedlings produced by outdoor sowings from mice.

FAR RIGHT *Once the seed has germinated and the seedlings are large enough to handle, they can be potted on.*

1 Sunflower seeds are good and large – easy enough to sow individually. (Dwarf varieties do have smaller seeds.)

2 Sow the seeds individually in pots or modules. Cover to their own depth with compost. Alternatively, sow them in drills outdoors. Space them 30–45cm (12–18in) apart, depending on the variety. Large types may need more room.

Lunaria annua

syn. *L. biennis* Honesty, satin flower Cruciferae

WHEN TO SOW
Late summer through to autumn, or spring.

PRE-TREATMENT
None necessary.

HOW TO SOW
In pots, trays or modules of standard seed compost topped with grit, perlite or vermiculite. Alternatively, sow in seed beds outdoors in spring.

GERMINATION
4–6 months.

TIME TILL FLOWERING
10 weeks–8 months, depending on when the seeds were sown.

ULTIMATE SIZE
90cm x 30cm (36in x 12in).

This hardy biennial is much beloved of flower arrangers – though not for its flowers. Purple, or, if you are lucky, white, and produced in spring, these are on the weedy side, but the seedheads that follow – translucent pearly white coins – are long-lasting and highly decorative. For white flowers, look for packeted seed of *Lunaria annua* var. *albiflora*.

why grow from seed

This is a plant that often seeds itself where it will in gardens, but for more control, especially if you want one of the selected forms, it is best to raise plants yourself for use in autumn borders or in a cutting border.

aftercare

Place containers outdoors to germinate, which may not occur until the following spring. Any seedlings that germinate should be kept in a cold frame over winter. Thin outdoor sowings as necessary. Transplant seedlings into their flowering positions when they are 10–15cm (4–6in) tall.

FAR RIGHT *Honesty seed cases have a pearly quality to them.*

1 When the seed pods are pearly white and have dried out completely, cut them from the plant. Gently crumble the cases to release the black seeds.

2 Sow the seeds in pots, trays or modules filled with standard seed compost and top with grit, perlite or vermiculite. Alternatively, sow in drills outdoors (spring only).

Matthiola incana

Gillyflower, stock Brassicaceae/Cruciferae

WHEN TO SOW
Spring to early summer; sow in autumn for early flowers the following year.

PRE-TREATMENT
None necessary.

HOW TO SOW
Sow in pots, trays or modules of standard seed compost topped with perlite or vermiculite. Early sowings should be kept at 13–18°C (55–64°F).

GERMINATION
8–12 days.

TIME TILL FLOWERING
10–12 weeks; autumn sowings will not flower until the following spring.

ULTIMATE SIZE
50cm x 30cm (20in x 12in); however, dwarf varieties are more compact.

These rewarding hardy annuals are sometimes referred to as 'ten-week stocks', because that's the time between sowing and flowering. This means that you can squeeze in three or even four crops a year. The colour range is wide – white, pink, cream, red and mauve, with some double and dwarf forms. Most are delicately scented, but to boost the fragrance mix in a few seeds of night-scented stock (*Matthiola bicornis*).

why grow from seed

These plants are actually perennials but deteriorate rapidly, so they are best treated as annuals or biennials and raised from seed each year.

aftercare

Early sowings made under cover should be potted on as they grow using soil-based compost (John Innes No.1 or No.2) and planted in their final positions when about 10cm (4in) tall. Protect autumn sowings made outdoors under a cloche. Late sowings made in pots can be brought into flower in winter if kept in a cool greenhouse.

FAR RIGHT *Matthiola seedlings develop quickly once germinated.*

1 Stock seeds are flat and large enough to be handled with ease. They should be sown flat.

2 Sow in pots, trays or modules, and lightly top with perlite or vermiculite. Seeds can also be sown in drills outdoors; space them about 30cm (12in) apart – a little less for dwarf varieties.

Myosotis sylvatica

Forget-me-not Boraginaceae

WHEN TO SOW
Early summer.

PRE-TREATMENT
None necessary.

HOW TO SOW
Sow in pots, trays or modules of standard seed compost and top with perlite or vermiculite. Alternatively, raise plants in drills outdoors.

GERMINATION
14–30 days.

TIME TILL FLOWERING
6 months.

ULTIMATE SIZE
30cm x 15cm (12in x 6in); some varieties are more compact.

Forget-me-nots, hardy biennials, are essential spring bedders, and the combination with pink tulips is a classic one. Check the seed packets carefully. There's a wider colour range than you might think, with some dramatic rich blues well as pink and white strains.

why grow from seed

These plants often seed themselves in gardens, but it's better to buy commercially produced seed each year. Though you can save your own seed, this tends to produce plants that are less robust and of poor colour.

aftercare

If you are raising the plants in containers, pot them on in soil-based compost (John Innes No.2). If you have sown the seed in a nursery bed outdoors, thin the seedlings as they grow. In either case, transfer them to their flowering positions in late winter to early spring. Be sure to space the plants correctly, allowing about 23cm (9in) between plants, as overcrowding can lead to problems with mildew.

FAR RIGHT *Seedlings can be potted on individually for growing on before planting out.*

1 Tip the shiny black seeds from the packet. The seeds are small, but you should be able to sow them individually.

2 Sow the seeds in pots, trays or modules filled with standard seed compost, then lightly top with perlite or vermiculite. Germinate the seeds outdoors.

Nicandra physalodes

Apple of Peru, shoo-fly Solanaceae

WHEN TO SOW
Spring or autumn.

PRE-TREATMENT
None necessary.

HOW TO SOW
Sow in pots, trays or modules
that are filled with standard
seed compost.

GERMINATION
10–14 days; autumn sowings
may not germinate till the
following spring.

TIME TILL FLOWERING
10–12 weeks.

ULTIMATE SIZE
90cm x 30cm (36in x 12in).

Like *Lunaria annua* (see page 116), this annual is grown less for its flowers, which are small in relation to the plant, than its beautiful seedheads. These impressive lanterns are initially green with a strong purple flush, then dry out and split to reveal polished black fruits.

why grow from seed

This is one of the few commonly grown annuals that is a pure species, not a developed strain. It is always worth saving a few seeds each autumn for sowing the following year.

aftercare

Pot on the seedlings individually, using soil-based compost (John Innes No.1 or No.2). Water and feed the developing plants regularly with a liquid fertiliser during the growing season. Overwinter seedlings that have emerged from a late sowing in a cold frame. Plant out the seedlings when they are about 15cm (6in) high.

FAR RIGHT *Shoo-fly seedheads ripen in late summer as the leaves begin to fade.*

1 Remove individual seedheads from the plant as they ripen. Gently open the papery seed cases to reveal the black, tomato-like fruits.

2 Squash the fruits to release the seeds. Wash the seed, then dry on absorbent kitchen paper. Either sow immediately or store for sowing the following spring.

Nicotiana

Tobacco plant Solanaceae

WHEN TO SOW
Throughout spring.

PRE-TREATMENT
None necessary.

HOW TO SOW
In pots, modules or trays of standard seed compost topped with perlite or vermiculite. Seed can also be sown outdoors but only when there is no longer any risk of night frosts.

GERMINATION
1–3 weeks.

TIME TILL FLOWERING
3–5 months.

ULTIMATE SIZE
30cm x 20cm (12in x 8in), more or less, depending on the seed strain.

A garden is not a garden without a liberal sprinkling of tobacco plants. True, in hot weather, the trumpet-like flowers hang from the sticky stems in a most dejected way, but as the temperature cools in the evening they suddenly perk up to release the most intoxicating incense fragrance. There are white, pink and magenta red forms, as well as a very cool lime green.

why grow from seed

In their country of origin – Mexico – these plants are perennial, but, as they can flower in the same year they are sown, they are always treated as half-hardy annuals in cooler climates.

aftercare

Prick out seedlings and pot them on as they grow using soil-based compost (John Innes No.1 or No.2). Water and feed with a liquid fertiliser until planting out, when there's no longer any risk of night frosts. Seeds can also be sown outdoors where the plants are to flower, but wait till you're sure there won't be any more frosts.

FAR RIGHT *Once seeds have germinated, the little plants grow quickly.*

1 Tip the seed from the packet. The seeds are small and tricky to sow individually. If you are sowing in spring, hold some back for a later sowing.

2 Sow in pinches between finger and thumb in pots or modules or in rows in trays filled with standard seed compost. Top with perlite or vermiculite. Keep early sowings made under glass at 18–21°C (64–70°F).

Nigella damascena

Love-in-a-mist Ranunculaceae

WHEN TO SOW
Spring; make autumn sowings for late spring flowers the following year.

PRE-TREATMENT
None necessary.

HOW TO SOW
In pots or trays of standard seed compost. Seed can also be sown in drills outdoors.

GERMINATION
10–25 days.

TIME TILL FLOWERING
12 weeks; autumn sowings will flower late the following spring.

ULTIMATE SIZE
50cm x 23cm (20in x 9in), more or less, depending on the seed strain.

These enchanting hardy annuals are essential in a cottage garden. Aside from the attractions of the blue, pink or white flowers, the seedheads are also appealing, and it is worth leaving some on the plants for their intrinsic value as well as for providing seed for the next year. The 'in-a-mist' of the common name refers to the ruff-like arrangement of filigree leaves that surround the flowers.

why grow from seed

These plants generally seed themselves in gardens, usually producing flowers in a range of colours. For isolated colours, buy seed of specific strains each year.

aftercare

Germinate the seed outdoors. If you have sown in containers, prick out the seedlings and pot them on as they grow in soil-based compost (John Innes No.1 or No.2). Water and feed them regularly with a liquid fertiliser until large enough to plant out – usually when they are about 10–15cm (4–6in) high. Thin seedlings sown in drills. Protect autumn sowings by placing containers in a cold frame. If you are growing them in a nursery bed, shield them from frost with a cloche over winter.

FAR RIGHT *Nigella seedheads rattle when they ripen, which happens usually from late summer onwards.*

1 Cut the seed cases from the plant when they are dry and fully ripe. If not fully dry, hang them upside down in a warm kitchen until they turn uniformly beige.

2 Carefully break open the seed cases to release the seeds. Either sow immediately or store the seed ready for sowing the following spring.

Oenothera biennis

Evening primrose Onagraceae

WHEN TO SOW
Autumn or spring.

PRE-TREATMENT
None necessary.

HOW TO SOW
Sow in pots, trays or modules of standard seed compost and top with grit, sharp sand, vermiculite or perlite. Seed can also be sown in drills in a nursery bed in spring.

GERMINATION
3–4 weeks.

TIME TILL FLOWERING
6–8 months. Early spring sowings in containers can flower the same year.

ULTIMATE SIZE
1m x 40cm (3ft x 16in).

The common name refers to this hardy biennial's most charming characteristic. As the sun begins to fade in early evening, the soft lemon yellow flowers suddenly unfurl like parasols before your very eyes. Romantics like to plant them by the garden gate to provide a fragrant greeting when they get home from work.

why grow from seed
This plant will happily seed itself, but, for more control, collect ripe seed and plant out the seedlings in the positions you want them to flower in.

aftercare
Prick out the seedlings, if you are growing in pots. Water and feed the seedlings with a liquid fertiliser and pot them on regularly until large enough to plant out – usually when they are about 15cm (6in) high. If autumn sowings germinate quickly, overwinter the seedlings in a cold frame. Thin sowings made outdoors as necessary. Move them to their flowering positions in autumn.

FAR RIGHT *Evening primrose seed cases are held almost vertically on the stems and split open at the top.*

1 Cut the flowered stems from the plant when the seed cases turn beige-brown and start to split open. Gently tap the seed cases in order to release the seeds.

2 Sow the seeds in pots, trays or modules filled with standard seed compost and top with grit, sharp sand, perlite or vermiculite. Place the containers outdoors. Alternatively, sow in drills outdoors (spring only).

Primula

Primrose Primulaceae

WHEN TO SOW
Late winter to midsummer.

PRE-TREATMENT
None necessary.

HOW TO SOW
Sow in pots or trays of standard
seed compost topped with
perlite or vermiculite.

GERMINATION
10–30 days.

TIME TILL FLOWERING
6–8 months.

ULTIMATE SIZE
15cm x 15cm (6in x 6in).

Primula is a huge genus made up mainly of perennials, as well as the charming plants discussed here – which are usually referred to as polyanthus. Actually these are also perennials, but for the most vivid colours treat them as hardy biennials and raise fresh stocks each year. Flowers are duller and smaller on older plants.

why grow from seed

While polyanthus are widely available in florists and garden centres at the turn of the year, it is much more economical to raise your own plants from seed.

aftercare

Remove the plastic covering once germination has occurred. Transplant the seedlings when large enough to handle and grow them on in pots or trays of soil-based compost (John Innes No.2). Feed with a liquid fertiliser and water when in full growth, but keep the plants cool. Keep them in the shade during hot weather in summer, then plant out in autumn.

FAR RIGHT *Pot the seedlings up individually once they become large enough.*

1 Tip out the seeds. As they are small, you may find it easier to hold them in a scrap of paper that has been folded in half to form a chute.

2 Surface sow the seeds in pots or trays then top the seeds lightly with a thin layer of perlite or vermiculite. Tent the sown seeds with clear plastic to maintain an even temperature, ideally 15–20°C (59–68°F).

Senecio cineraria

syn. *Cineraria maritima* Asteraceae/Compositae

This half-hardy foliage plant makes ideal edging material to a large border or works as a foil to more brightly coloured plants in containers and windowboxes. Remove any flowers that may form. For the best leaf colour, plant in poor, well-drained soil in full sun – too many nutrients can turn the leaves green.

why grow from seed

Actually a shrub in its native Mediterranean, this is a plant that really looks its best only in its youth. That and the fact that it is not reliably hardy mean that it's always best to raise fresh plants from seed annually.

aftercare

Keep the pots at 18–20°C (64–68°F). When the seeds have germinated, remove any covering and grow the seedlings on in cooler conditions. Pot up the seedlings when they are large enough to handle. Water and feed with a liquid fertiliser regularly. Plant them out when they are 10–15cm (4–6in) high, when there is no longer any danger of hard frosts.

FAR RIGHT *Seedlings can be grown on in modules until they are large enough to plant out.*

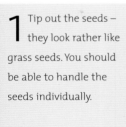

1 Tip out the seeds – they look rather like grass seeds. You should be able to handle the seeds individually.

2 Surface sow in pots, trays or modules filled with standard seed compost. Cover with a light layer of perlite or vermiculite, then seal in a clear plastic bag.

Viola

Pansy Violaceae

WHEN TO SOW
Mid- to late winter.

PRE-TREATMENT
Scarify the seed prior to sowing.

HOW TO SOW
In pots or trays of standard seed compost topped with grit, sharp sand, perlite or vermiculite.

GERMINATION
2–3 weeks.

TIME TILL FLOWERING
4–6 months.

ULTIMATE SIZE
15cm x 15cm (6in x 6in).

Few hardy annual have the appeal of pansies, with their charming 'faces' in a range of velvety colours – and white and cream, of course. While it's possible to sow throughout the year for non-stop flowering, it's easiest just to raise plants for summer planting schemes.

why grow from seed

Essential for windowboxes, hanging baskets and containers, it is much more economical to raise these plants from seed than buy them as bedding plants. But leave winter pansies to the professionals. These have to be germinated in summer, at a time when it's difficult for amateurs to replicate the low temperatures necessary for raising the plants.

aftercare

Unlike many annual, pansies need cool conditions to germinate. Keep the seed at no higher than 10°C (50°F) until germinated, then grow on outdoors in a cold frame. Pot them on as they grow using soil-based compost (John Innes No.1 or No.2). Water and feed regularly with a liquid fertiliser until large enough to plant out – when they are about 5cm (2in) tall.

FAR RIGHT *Seedlings can be grown on in trays or modules before they are planted out.*

1 Tip out the seeds. It's not immediately obvious, but the seeds have a coat that can inhibit germination.

2 Rub the seeds lightly between sheets of sandpaper to break down the seed coat and accelerate germination. Sow in pots or trays of standard seed compost. Top with grit, sharp sand, perlite or vermiculite.

vegetables and herbs

Onions

Allium cepa Liliaceae

WHEN TO SOW
Late winter to early spring.

PRE-TREATMENT
None necessary.

HOW TO SOW
In trays, pots or modules filled with standard seed compost, topped with grit. Alternatively, sow in drills outdoors.

GERMINATION
5–10 days.

TIME TILL HARVESTING
5–6 months or longer.

ULTIMATE SIZE
30cm x 10cm (12in x 4in), more or less, depending on the variety.

Essential in cooking, onions need a long growing season – but the rewards are considerable. Properly dried off in summer, they can be stored over winter so you will never be short of a bulb for stews and roasts. Onions are commonly grown from 'sets' – small onions that have been raised commercially. But you can also grow your own from seed.

conditions required

Onions do best in a fertile, well-drained, not too heavy soil. Carry out any soil improvement at least three months before sowing, as onions do not like the high nitrogen levels associated with recently manured ground.

aftercare

Prick out seedlings growing in containers and grow them on in pots of soil-based compost (John Innes No.2 or No.3) until large enough to plant out. Outdoors, seed can be encouraged to germinate by covering with a cloche or horticultural fleece. Thin the seedlings to 10–15cm (4–6in) apart, depending on the variety.

FAR RIGHT *A young onion ready for transplanting.*

1 Onion seed is easy to handle, and, like all parts of the plant, carries that distinctive smell. Fill pots, trays or modules with seed compost.

2 Surface sow the seed, then top with grit. Put the seeds in a cold frame outdoors. Onion seed can also be sown in drills outdoors. Seed germinates at temperatures above 7°C (45°F).

Beetroot

Beta vulgaris subsp. *vulgaris* Chenopodiaceae

WHEN TO SOW
Early spring to midsummer.

PRE-TREATMENT
None necessary.

HOW TO SOW
In pots, trays or modules filled with standard seed compost or in drills outdoors.

GERMINATION
2–3 weeks.

TIME TILL HARVESTING
12 weeks, but small roots can also be pulled before then.

ULTIMATE SIZE
10–20cm x 2.5–7.5cm (4–8in x 1–3in), depending on when the beetroot is harvested.

Beetroot is one of the latest super foods, an excellent source of fibre and reputed to be high in anti-carcinogens. Harvest when small for eating raw, or wait until they reach the size of tennis balls and bake or boil. Sow at 14-day intervals from spring onwards to ensure a steady supply of youngsters throughout summer and autumn. Most people discard the green tops, but please don't. Cooked as you would spinach or cabbage they are tasty and iron-rich.

conditions required

Beetroot does best on fertile, fairly light soil that has been recently improved or treated with a nitrogen-high fertiliser. It can also be grown in containers.

aftercare

Seed germinates at temperatures no lower than 7°C (45°F). Keep early sowings in containers in a cold frame. Water them if they show signs of drying out. Cover seedlings outdoors with a cloche or horticultural fleece for early crops.

FAR RIGHT *Beetroot tops can also be eaten, and are best while they are still young.*

1 Beetroot seeds are large, nobbly and easy to sow. If you are sowing outdoors, sow at the distance recommended for the variety, 5cm (2in) apart or less if you are intending to harvest the roots small. There should be no need to thin the seedlings.

2 You can also sow seeds in pots, trays or modules filled with standard seed compost for planting out later or for potting on into larger containers.

Cauliflower

Brassica oleracea Botrytis Group Brassicaceae/Cruciferae

WHEN TO SOW
Spring to autumn, depending on the variety.

PRE-TREATMENT
None necessary.

HOW TO SOW
In pots, trays or modules filled with standard seed compost, topped with perlite or vermiculite. Seed can also be sown in drills outdoors.

GERMINATION
1–2 weeks.

TIME TILL HARVESTING
From 12 weeks for mini-cauliflowers; overwintering plants may need up to 6 months or more for the heads to develop.

ULTIMATE SIZE
30cm x 45cm (12in x 18in).

Cauliflowers are beautiful vegetables. Besides the commonly seen creamy white heads, you will also find varieties with purple or green curds. By sowing in succession it's possible to have cauliflowers for the kitchen all year round. Mini-cauliflowers are harvested when the curds are still small.

conditions required

Cauliflowers do best in moderately fertile, fairly heavy soil. Some varieties do well on less fertile soils.

aftercare

To germinate seed sown in containers, keep at 15–20°C (59–68°F). Grow on the seedlings in a cold frame in containers filled with soil-based compost (John Innes No.2 or No.3). Water if the compost shows signs of drying out. Plant out early sowings in mid-spring to early summer. The final planting distance should be around 45cm (18in) or more depending on the variety. Tighter spacing can be used for mini-cauliflowers. Late sowings in pots should be overwintered in a cold frame. Overwintering plants sown outdoors should be protected from frost with a cloche or horticultural fleece.

FAR RIGHT *Cauliflower seedlings that have just been pricked out.*

1 Cauliflower seeds are small and spherical. To prepare for sowing, fill pots, trays or modules with standard seed compost. Lightly press the seed into the compost surface.

2 Top with a light covering of perlite or vermiculite. This method is recommended for sowings in early spring and autumn. Sowings from mid-spring through summer can be made outdoors *in situ*.

Sweet peppers

Capsicum annuum Grossum Group Solanaceae

Sweet peppers are actually fruits – and like most fruits they need to bask in the summer sun to ripen fully. The riper they are the sweeter the flavour. Unripe fruits are green, gradually turning to red, yellow or purple. Sweet peppers are tender plants that need a long growing season, so start them off as early as you can.

conditions required

These tropical plants can be grown outdoors only in warm areas and appreciate fertile, well-drained soil. In cool areas, they are best treated as container plants and grown in a greenhouse or polytunnel or near to a warm wall outside.

aftercare

Once the seeds have germinated, keep them at a minimum temperature of 15°C (59°F). Pot them on individually using soil-based compost (John Innes No.2 or No.3). Plant out only when all danger of frost has passed. Water peppers in containers regularly and feed with a tomato fertiliser. Support plants with canes if necessary.

FAR RIGHT *A sweet pepper seedling that is ready for potting on.*

1 Pepper seeds are fairly large and should be sown individually. Fill pots, trays or modules with standard seed compost.

2 Lightly press the seeds onto the compost surface, then cover with a light layer of perlite or vermiculite. Germinate the seed at 20–25°C (68–77°F).

Pumpkins and squashes

Cucurbita spp. Cucurbitaceae

WHEN TO SOW
Mid- to late spring.

PRE-TREATMENT
Soaking seed for up to 24 hours before sowing can accelerate the germination process.

HOW TO SOW
In pots or modules filled with standard seed compost topped with perlite or vermiculite.

GERMINATION
5–10 days.

TIME TILL HARVESTING
12–20 weeks.

ULTIMATE SIZE
2m x 2m (6½ft x 6½ft), more or less, depending on the variety; bushy types are more compact.

These vigorous, tender plants produce large fruits that are excellent for use in winter soups. Either allow the plants to trail, or train them upwards on tripods. Once cut from the plant, a pumpkin can be kept for six to eight weeks.

conditions required
Pumpkins and squashes do best in fertile, moist but well-drained soil in full sun.

aftercare
Keep the seeds at 20–25°C (68–77°F) until they have germinated. Grow on in soil-based compost (John Innes No.2 or No.3), watering frequently, then move to their fruiting positions when all danger of frost has passed. Pumpkins and squashes can also be grown *in situ* but you should sow only when there is no longer any risk of frost. For the best crops, keep the plants well watered while the fruits are forming.

FAR RIGHT *Seedlings will be ready to pot on 7–14 days after germinating.*

1 The seeds are large and easy to handle. Either sow straight from the packet or soak in water for no longer than 24 hours to speed up germination.

2 Sow the seeds either *in situ* or start them off in pots or modules filled with standard seed compost. They can be sown individually. Cover with perlite or vermiculite.

Cut-and-come-again lettuces

Lactuca sativa Compositae

WHEN TO SOW
Sow in succession from early spring to midsummer; later sowings can also be made for cropping under cover.

PRE-TREATMENT
None necessary.

HOW TO SOW
Sow in pots, trays or modules filled with standard seed compost topped with perlite or vermiculite, or in a finely raked seed bed outdoors.

GERMINATION
10–14 days.

TIME TILL HARVESTING
8 weeks or less, depending on the speed of growth.

ULTIMATE SIZE
15–25cm x 15–25cm (6–10in x 6–10in), depending on the variety.

Cut-and-come-again lettuces are an ideal crop if you have limited space, as only a few plants are needed to produce a daily crop of fresh leaves over several weeks. Regular cutting actually encourages the plants to produce new leaves.

conditions required

Lettuces need reliably moist, fertile soil in an open or lightly shaded situation. They are also an excellent choice for containers. They do not do well in hot conditions, which encourage the plants to run to seed, or bolt, spoiling the flavour. Some varieties, however, are bolt-resistant.

aftercare

Seed germinates at low temperatures, so additional protection is not required. Prick out the seedlings into pots filled with soil-based compost (John Innes No.2 or No.3). Water them if the compost shows signs of drying out. Thin sowings made outdoors (the thinnings can be washed and added whole to salads). The final spacing of plants should be 15–30cm (6–12in), depending on the variety.

FAR RIGHT *Seedlings should be thinned. You can eat the thinnings in salads.*

1 Shake the seeds from the packet. They are large enough to sow individually. Sow the seeds in pots, trays or modules filled with standard seed compost.

2 Top the seeds with a layer or perlite or vermiculite. Place the pots outdoors. Sowings can also be made outdoors *in situ*.

Parsley

Petroselinum crispum Apiaceae/Umbelliferae

WHEN TO SOW
In succession from early spring to late summer; later sowings can also be made with protection.

PRE-TREATMENT
Soak seeds in hot water overnight before sowing.

HOW TO SOW
Sow in pots, trays or modules of standard seed compost, topped with perlite or vermiculite, or in drills outdoors.

GERMINATION
3–6 weeks, sometimes less with overnight soaking.

TIME TILL HARVESTING
From 8–12 weeks onwards.

ULTIMATE SIZE
30cm x 30cm (12in x 12in).

Parsley, a rich source of vitamin C, is one of the most rewarding crops to grow. It makes a great edging plant to a vegetable plot – or even in the flower garden – and you can cut from the plants throughout the summer. If you're lucky, plants may survive the winter. Look for flat-leaved varieties – they have superior flavour to the curly-leaf types.

conditions required

Parsley prefers a fertile, well-drained soil in sun or light shade. It can be also be grown successfully in pots or hanging baskets.

aftercare

Germinate seed in containers at 18–20°C (64–68°F). Grow on in pots of soil-based compost (John Innes No.2). Water if the compost shows signs of drying out. For sowings made outdoors, thin the seedlings to about 23cm (9in) apart. Harvest the leaves regularly to keep the plants producing fresh leaves and to prevent them from flowering and running to seed. Plants in containers or hanging baskets should be fed with a seaweed-based fertiliser.

FAR RIGHT *Pricked out parsley seedlings ready for potting up.*

1 The seed is easy to handle, so can be sown individually. Fill pots, trays or modules with standard seed compost.

2 Surface sow the seed, then lightly top with a covering of perlite or vermiculite. Alternatively, sow the seed outdoors in drills from late spring onwards.

French beans, dwarf beans

Phaseolus vulgaris Leguminosae

WHEN TO SOW
Spring; dwarf forms can also be sown in midsummer for autumn cropping.

PRE-TREATMENT
None necessary.

HOW TO SOW
In pots or modules filled with standard seed compost, topped with perlite or vermiculite.

GERMINATION
5–10 days with protection; 2–3 weeks outdoors.

TIME TILL HARVESTING
8–10 weeks.

ULTIMATE SIZE
2m x 45cm (6½ft x 18in), climbing forms; 30–45cm x 30cm (12–18in x 12in), dwarf forms.

This is one instance when it is just about worth leaving a few beans on the plant to ripen and give you seed for the following year. But don't do this too often, as certain diseases can enter the seed via the open flower. It's best to buy fresh seed that is guaranteed disease-free every two or three years. Make two sowings for extended crops.

conditions required

French beans are half-hardy and need a warm, sheltered, sunny site and fertile, well-drained soil. They do not do well on heavy soils. Dwarf varieties can be grown in containers.

aftercare

Germinate the seeds at 10°C (50°F) or higher. Pot up the seedlings using soil-based compost (John Innes No.2 or No.3). Water them if the compost shows signs of drying out. Plant them out when there is no longer any danger of frost, spacing them 15–38cm (6–15in) apart, depending on the variety. Seed can also be sown in its cropping position. Protect early sowings with a cloche or horticultural fleece.

FAR RIGHT *As the seed cases dry out in autumn, the seeds inside swell up and ripen.*

1 Split the seed cases to expose the seeds. Remove the seeds from the cases. Alternatively, you can buy fresh packeted seed for sowing.

2 Sow the seeds individually in pots or modules. Cover the seeds to their own depth with standard seed compost, then top with perlite or vermiculite. Alternatively, they can be sown *in situ* outdoors.

Radishes

Raphanus sativus Cruciferae

Radishes can be sown in succession over a long period, and can be harvested when small or left to develop to the size of marbles or slightly larger. Keep sowing and harvesting them. Left in the ground too long, they turn corky and lose flavour. Eat them as soon after picking as you can. Wash them first, of course, but they should still have the scent of the earth on them. They are one of the easiest vegetables to grow.

conditions required

Radishes do best in a sunny, open spot, in fertile, moist but well-drained soil.

aftercare

Prick out the seedlings and grow them on in soil-based compost (John Innes No.2 or No.3). Water them if the compost shows signs of drying out. Plant out when large enough, spacing them 10–15cm (4–6in) apart, depending on the variety. Outdoors, thin seedlings to the appropriate spacing – 10–15cm (4–6in) apart.

FAR RIGHT *You can eat the entire radish apart from the white roots.*

1 Radish seeds are spherical and easy to handle. They can be sown *in situ* outdoors or in trays, pots or modules filled with standard seed compost.

2 If you are sowing in containers, lightly press the seed onto the compost surface. Top the seeds with a light covering of perlite or vermiculite. Place the containers outdoors.

Aubergine, eggplant

Solanum melongena Solanaceae

WHEN TO SOW
Late winter to early spring.

PRE-TREATMENT
Soak the seed for 12 hours
before sowing.

HOW TO SOW
Sow in pots or modules filled
with standard seed compost and
top with perlite or vermiculite.

GERMINATION
7–14 days.

TIME TILL HARVESTING
6–8 months.

ULTIMATE SIZE
1.1–2m x 45cm (3½–6½ft x 18in).

Aubergines, or eggplants, are tender fruiting vegetables that need high temperatures to crop successfully. They need a long growing season so, to be sure of getting a good yield, start the seeds off early. They do well in large containers or growing bags, either placed outdoors in a sunny, sheltered spot or in an unheated greenhouse. Besides the typical purple varieties there are also attractive white-fruited forms.

conditions required

Aubergines need fertile, well-drained soil and should be grown in a warm, sheltered site.

aftercare

Transplant the seedlings individually into 7.5cm (3in) pots filled with soil-based compost (John Innes No.2 or No.3). When the roots fill the pots, pot them up into large pots filled with similar compost or into growing bags. Water the plants regularly and feed with tomato fertiliser or some other product formulated for fruiting vegetables. Stake the plants if necessary.

FAR RIGHT *These aubergine seedlings are ready for potting on.*

1 Aubergine seeds are fairly small, but you should be able to handle them easily. Fill pots or modules with standard seed compost.

2 Sow the seeds evenly on the compost surface then top them with a thin layer of perlite or vermiculite. Germinate the seeds at 15–20°C (59–68°F).

Spinach

Spinacia oleracea Chenopodiaceae

WHEN TO SOW
Spring to early summer; late summer to early autumn under glass for winter crops.

PRE-TREATMENT
None necessary.

HOW TO SOW
In pots, trays or modules of standard seed compost topped with perlite or vermiculite. Alternatively, sow outdoors in drills.

GERMINATION
2–3 weeks.

TIME TILL HARVESTING
6 weeks (spring sowings); late sowings take up to 10 weeks to mature.

ULTIMATE SIZE
25cm x 25cm (10in x 10in).

Spinach is a great source of iron and vitamin C, and the crops you grow yourself at home are far tastier than anything you can buy in the supermarket or at the greengrocers. It is one of those crops that are best eaten as quickly after cutting as possible. Just a few plants should provide leaves for cutting every day throughout the summer.

conditions required

Grow spinach in fertile, well-drained soil in sun or light shade.

aftercare

Seed can be germinated outdoors. Prick out seedlings started in containers and transplant into soil-based compost (John Innes No.2 or No.3). Keep the seedlings well watered. Plant out when large enough, spacing the plants 15cm (6in) apart. Thin sowings made outdoors to the same distance. Winter crops are best grown under a cloche or in a polytunnel.

FAR RIGHT *Pot on the seedlings as they grow.*

1 The spherical seeds are nice and large, so can be sown individually. Prepare pots, trays or modules by filling with standard seed compost.

2 Lightly press the seeds into the compost surface, then top with perlite or vermiculite. Seed can also be sown outdoors in drills.

Sweetcorn

Zea mays Gramineae/Poaceae

WHEN TO SOW
Late spring.

PRE-TREATMENT
None necessary.

HOW TO SOW
Sow in pots or modules filled with standard seed compost topped with perlite or vermiculite. They can also be sown directly in the ground where they are to crop, once all danger of frosts has passed.

GERMINATION
7–10 days, sometimes longer for seed sown outdoors.

TIME TILL HARVESTING
4–5 months.

ULTIMATE SIZE
1.1–1.2m x 45cm (3½–4ft x 18in).

The golden yellow cobs of corn are unmistakable, though white and bicoloured varieties are also available. They need a long growing season for the cobs to ripen fully. Corn is wind pollinated, so it's best to arrange the plants in blocks of four or five rather than rows to ensure good cropping.

conditions required

Sweetcorn is a tender crop that needs fertile, well-drained soil in a sheltered site in full sun.

aftercare

Germinate the seed at 20–30°C (68–86°F). Grow on in containers filled with soil-based compost (John Innes No.2 or No.3) and plant out when large enough, spacing the plants 30–45cm (12–18in) apart, depending on the variety. Use the same spacings for sowings made *in situ*.

FAR RIGHT *A pair of sweetcorn seedlings.*

1 Sweetcorn seeds are distinctive and instantly recognisable. You can either sow them *in situ* or start them off in containers filled with standard seed compost.

2 Press the seed lightly into the compost surface. Cover to their own depth with compost, then top with perlite or vermiculite.

the indoor garden

Mustard and other sprouting seeds

Brassica hirta and other species Cruciferae

Even if you think you cannot grow anything from seed, have a go with mustard, cress and other sprouting seeds, as it is almost impossible to fail. You can buy special jars for germinating the seeds, but these aren't necessary. A number of sprouting plants, including the highly nutritious adzuki beans, can be raised using the simple method detailed below.

why grow from seed
Seeds germinate in a matter of days, so it is possible to have a fresh supply for harvesting all year round.

aftercare
Keep the seeds in a warm place, around 20°C (68°F), such as on a warm kitchen windowsill. Water the growing medium regularly to make sure it stays evenly moist – it must not be allowed to dry out. Some seeds can be sprouted in an airing cupboard.

FAR RIGHT *You can harvest the sprouting seeds within a few days of sowing them.*

1 Tip some seed from the packet. It is large enough to be handled with ease. Sow only as much as will serve your immediate needs, reserving the rest.

2 Lay sheets of blotting paper, absorbent kitchen paper or cotton wool on a seed tray or a saucer. Dampen this, then set the seeds on top. Press down gently to make sure they are in contact with the growing medium.

CACTI

Various species Cactaceae

WHEN TO SOW
Late winter to late spring.

PRE-TREATMENT
None necessary, though large
seed can be stratified in the
fridge for 2 days before sowing.

HOW TO SOW
In small pots filled with cactus
compost or standard seed
compost with added grit or
sharp sand.

GERMINATION
2 weeks or longer, depending on
the species.

TIME TILL FLOWERING
3–5 years, or longer.

ULTIMATE SIZE
5cm x 5cm (2in x 2in) or larger
(globular cacti); columnar types
can be up to 1.2m (4ft) tall or
even more.

Cacti are a large group of plants mainly from the New World. Most are spiny, and range from small, golf ball-like plants to larger, branching plants that are almost tree-like. The most effective method of display is to group several different species together to create a mini cactus garden. Packeted seed is usually of a number of different species.

why grow from seed
New species are still being discovered and seed is the best way of increasing their availability rapidly in cultivation.

aftercare
Once germinated, remove the pots from the propagator or their plastic tent and grow the seedlings on in normal glasshouse conditions – ie with a minimum temperature of 10°C (50°F). Leave the seedlings undisturbed for about three months to allow the roots to develop. The visible part of the plant will not grow much during this time. Pot the seedlings up individually when they are large enough to handle easily. Water them regularly, but allow the compost to become almost dry between waterings. Feed with a cactus fertiliser when they are in growth between spring and summer.

FAR RIGHT *This cactus seedling is now large enough for growing in its own pot.*

1 For ease of sowing mix the seed, which can be tiny, with a small amount of sharp sand on a piece of paper.

2 Surface sow the seed evenly in pots of cactus compost or standard seed compost topped with fine grit or sharp sand. If you do not have a propagator, tent the pot with a clear plastic bag. Keep the sown seed at 19–27°C (66–81°F).

Citrus

Citrus spp. Rutaceae

WHEN TO SOW
Summer.

PRE-TREATMENT
None necessary.

HOW TO SOW
In pots that have been filled with standard seed compost.

GERMINATION
3–4 weeks.

TIME TILL FLOWERING
5 years or more.

ULTIMATE SIZE
2m x 2m (6½ft x 6½ft) or more; plants can be kept smaller by regular pruning.

Citrus make attractive plants for the house or conservatory, with glossy evergreen leaves, delightfully scented flowers and edible – honestly – fruits. Commercially, citrus are usually grown from seed even for fruit production, so you can expect your seedlings to flower and even fruit. Without a long, hot summer, however, these are unlikely to ripen sufficiently and will be too acidic to eat raw, but you may be able to make some passable marmalade.

why grow from seed
Seed is a very reliable method of raising new citrus plants.

aftercare
Keep the seed at around 18°C (64°F) until germinated. Pot up the seedlings individually using soil-based compost (John Innes No.2 or No.3) with added sharp sand or horticultural grit. Keep the seedlings in a light position but shaded from hot sun, water them regularly and feed with a liquid fertiliser when in full growth. Water sparingly in winter.

FAR RIGHT *The kumquat is an unusual citrus and usually has large seeds.*

1 Cut the fruits in half to expose the seeds. Carefully extract the seeds with the point of a knife, discarding any you may have damaged when making the cut.

2 Wash the seeds in water. Dry them on absorbent kitchen paper. All the seeds can be sown, even little wrinkled ones. Sow in pots filled with standard seed compost.

Mango

Mangifera indica Anacardiaceae

WHEN TO SOW
When the seed is fresh, which is when the fruit is soft and edible.

PRE-TREATMENT
Rub the seed with sandpaper to roughen the surface, then soak in warm water for up to 2 weeks prior to sowing. Change the water regularly.

HOW TO SOW
In pots that have been filled with standard seed compost.

GERMINATION
3–6 weeks.

TIME TILL FLOWERING
3–5 years.

ULTIMATE SIZE
15–18m x 12m (50–60ft x 40ft); plants in containers will be much smaller.

In their natural state mangoes are impressive trees, whose branches droop down under the weight of the ripening fruits. While a plant is unlikely to flower and fruit in cultivation, it is well worth sowing a seed just to observe the germination process.

why grow from seed

With their glossy green leaves, mangoes make attractive houseplants. They are not widely available, so it is best to raise your own plants from seed.

aftercare

Sow the seeds individually in pots filled with standard seed compost. Cover each seed to a depth of about 2.5cm (1in). Keep the seeds in a propagator at 20–25°C (68–77°F) until they germinate. Water if the compost looks dry. (The seeds should not be allowed to dry out.) Once germinated, grow them on in slightly cooler conditions, such as on a sunny windowsill. Pot them on when the roots fill the pot, using soil-based compost (John Innes No.3). Water them freely when in full growth and feed with a general liquid fertiliser.

FAR RIGHT *Mango fruits are large but each contains only one seed.*

1 Cut down either side of the fruit to expose the stone. Cut the rest of the flesh away from the fruit and scrape off any residue with a knife.

2 Wash the stone in water to get rid of as much of the remaining flesh as possible. Dry the stone, then rub it with sandpaper. Mango seed should be sown fresh, immediately after soaking (see Pre-treatment, above left). It is not suitable for storing.

Basil

Ocimum basilicum Labiatae/Lamiaceae

WHEN TO SOW
Early spring to summer.

PRE-TREATMENT
None necessary.

HOW TO SOW
In pots, trays or modules filled with standard seed compost and topped with sharp sand, perlite or vermiculite.

GERMINATION
1–2 weeks.

TIME TILL FLOWERING
8–10 weeks, but it is best to prevent flowering by regularly picking the leaves.

ULTIMATE SIZE
30cm x 20cm (12in x 8in), more or less, depending on the variety.

This delicious herb, which is essential in Mediterranean cooking, is easily grown indoors on a kitchen windowsill – as long as you protect it from strong sunlight in summer. There is a wide range of cultivars, including some with purple leaves and others with tiny, intensely flavoured leaves. Experiment with varieties until you find the one – or several – that pleases you best.

why grow from seed
While growing plants are widely available in supermarkets, the flavour cannot compare with that of plants that have been raised from seed at home.

aftercare
Grow on the seedlings in slightly cooler conditions. Pot them on when they are large enough to handle, using soil-based compost (John Innes No.2). Water regularly, but only in the mornings. (Water in the evening and the drop in temperature overnight can lead to rotting.) Feed with an organic, seaweed-based fertiliser.

FAR RIGHT *Seedlings can be potted up individually or you can put several in a large pot.*

1 Tip the seed out. You should be able to handle individual seeds. Fill the pots, trays or modules with standard seed compost.

2 Surface sow the seeds thinly. Top the seeds with a layer of sharp sand, perlite or vermiculite. Germinate the seeds at around 20°C (68°F).

Pelargonium

Pelargonium Geraniaceae

WHEN TO SOW
Late winter.

PRE-TREATMENT
None necessary.

HOW TO SOW
In pots, trays or modules filled with standard seed compost. Cover the seeds to their own depth with compost and then top with sharp sand, perlite or vermiculite.

GERMINATION
3–21 days.

TIME TILL FLOWERING
3–4 months.

ULTIMATE SIZE
15–30cm x 15–30cm (6–12in x 6–12in), depending on the particular variety.

These tender perennials are grown for their seemingly unending succession of red, pink or white flowers in summer. Keep the plants in a conservatory over winter, and they can be persuaded to carry on flowering throughout the coldest months.

why grow from seed
While it is easy to increase stocks from cuttings, over time plants deteriorate and the amount of good cuttings material declines. For the overall health of your collection, it is always worthwhile producing new plants from seed. There are many excellent F1 and F2 cultivars.

aftercare
Keep the seeds at 21–24°C (70–75°F) until germinated. Grow on the seedlings at a slightly lower temperature but aim to keep this constant, as a sudden drop can make seedlings die off. Pot on the seedlings into soil-based compost (John Innes No.2) with added horticultural grit, sharp sand, perlite or vermiculite. Water them regularly and feed with a liquid fertiliser.

FAR RIGHT *Pot up the seedlings individually when they are about 5–10cm (2–4in) high.*

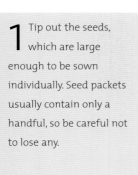

1 Tip out the seeds, which are large enough to be sown individually. Seed packets usually contain only a handful, so be careful not to lose any.

2 Sow the seed evenly spaced in pots, trays or modules of standard seed compost. Cover the seeds to their own depth with compost, or a layer of sharp sand, perlite or vermiculite.

Avocado

Persea americana Lauraceae

WHEN TO SOW
When the seed is ripe, which is when the fruit is soft and edible.

PRE-TREATMENT
Soak the seed in hot water for about 30 minutes before sowing (optional).

HOW TO SOW
Either sow in pots of soil-based compost, with the nose of the seed about 1cm (½in) above the compost surface, or germinate in water as shown.

GERMINATION
4 weeks or more.

TIME TILL FLOWERING
7 years, though plants in cultivation may be reluctant to flower.

ULTIMATE SIZE
2m x 30cm (6½ft x 12in) when pot grown; plants grown commercially in subtropical climates for fruit production are usually much larger.

It's fun to try growing an avocado plant at home. It seems miraculous that the rather hard, big stones will produce a plant. Avocado is unlikely to fruit at home, and tends to develop a long straight stem with just a pair of leaves at the top. If this happens, throw it out and start again. If you compost your avocado pits, you may find them germinating in the compost heap.

why grow from seed
You are unlikely to find avocado plants in the shops – they are of little intrinsic beauty. The charm lies in the ease with which the stones can be persuaded to produce a living plant.

aftercare
Keep the seed at room temperature (20–25°C/68–77°F). A place on a warm kitchen windowsill is ideal. If germinating in water, replace the water regularly so it does not turn green. Once germinated, pot on into soil-based compost (John Innes No.2 or No.3) with added slow-release fertiliser. Water freely and mist daily when in full growth in spring and summer.

FAR RIGHT *Avocado stones, or pits, can be germinated in water.*

1 Cut the fruit in half, taking care not to damage the stone within. Excavate the stone from the flesh with a teaspoon.

2 Clean off any remaining flesh from the stone. You can slip the papery coat from the stone, though this is not necessary. Suspend the stone over water so that the base of the stone is just in contact with the surface (see picture opposite for how to do this).

Date

Phoenix dactylifera Arecaceae/Palmae

Date palms are commonly grown as street
trees in the Mediterranean and other balmy
places in the world. In a warm climate they
make large, imposing plants, but in the short
to medium term they are ideal as pot plants
for the home or conservatory with their stiff,
architectural leaves.

why grow from seed

Fresh dates are something of a winter treat. Instead of throwing
away the stones, why not try sowing a few? They are easily
germinated in warm conditions, and this is a much more successful
method of propagation than attempting to take cuttings.

aftercare

Keep the seeds in humid conditions, ideally in a closed propagator,
at 25–28°C (77–82°F). Keep the propagator in a light position.
Monitor the seeds carefully. Water as necessary to prevent the
compost drying out and ventilate the unit if the temperature
climbs too high. Pot on the seedlings once germinated using soil-
based compost (John Innes No.2 or No.3) with added grit, perlite or
vermiculite and slow-release fertiliser and gradually acclimatise
them to life outside the propagator. Grow them on in a light
position that is shaded from direct sunlight.

FAR RIGHT *Fresh dates are
usually imported in
mid-winter.*

1 Either cut open the
dates or squeeze them
at one end to extract the
seed. Each fruit contains
one seed. Scrape off any
flesh clinging to the seeds.

2 Wash the seeds in water
as they are usually sticky.
Then sow individually in deep
pots. (If you need to store the
seeds, wrap them in damp
kitchen paper or cotton wool
and seal in a plastic bag. Seed
should be kept for no longer
than eight weeks.)

Solenostemon scutellarioides

syn. *Coleus blumei* var. *verschaffeltii* Coleus, flame nettle Labiatae/Lamiacea

WHEN TO SOW
Any time of year, though
winter sowings may be slow
to germinate.

PRE-TREATMENT
None necessary.

HOW TO SOW
In pots, trays or modules filled
with standard seed compost.

GERMINATION
10–20 days.

TIME TILL FLOWERING
10–12 weeks, but flowers are
best removed.

ULTIMATE SIZE
45cm x 45cm (18in x 18in); some
varieties are more compact.

These are excellent foliage plants for growing on a shady windowsill. The leaves are boldly marked with bronze, yellow and a blackish brown. They are often used as summer bedding plants outdoors but they are actually shrubby perennials that keep their leaves over winter.

why grow from seed

While it's possible to increase favourite plants by cuttings, the quality deteriorates over time and it is always best to raise new plants from seed. Most seedlings vary considerably in their leaf markings, but all are attractive.

aftercare

Germinate the seeds at 21–24°C (70–75°F). When the seedlings are large enough, pot them on individually in pots of soil-based compost (John Innes No.2 or No.3). Water them freely when in active growth and feed with a liquid fertiliser. Shade the plants from direct sunlight at all times.

FAR RIGHT *Prick out
seedlings when large
enough to handle.*

1 Tip out the seed, which is tiny, from the packet. If you cannot handle individual seed easily, you can sow them in small pinches.

2 Surface sow the seed in small pots, trays or modules filled with standard seed compost. Put the seeds in a clear plastic bag. Alternatively, sow in a tray with a clear plastic lid.

plant portraits

104-105

106-107

110-

112-113

114-115

116-

118-119

120-121

122-

124-125

126-127

128-1

130-131

132-133

134-

138-139

140-141

142-1

144-145

146-147

148-149

150-151

152-153

154-155

156-157

158-159

160-161

164-165

166-167

168-169

170-171

172-173

174-175

176-177

178-179

180-181

Glossary

Anther The part of a flower that produces pollen.

Berry A pulpy or fleshy fruit.

Bract A modified leaf at the base of a flower.

Cloche A portable unit, usually made of glass or clear plastic, placed over young or vulnerable plants that are growing in open ground.

Compost A growing medium for container plants. Only proprietary composts are suitable for seed sowing and growing on young plants. They are based on loam ('soil-based'), peat or coir. Some are specifically for seed sowing. *See also* garden compost.

Cone The seed-bearing structure produced by conifers, usually comprising woody bracts.

Cotyledon The first leaf that is produced on germination of a seed.

Dormancy Of seeds, meaning alive but not active or growing.

Drill A shallow trench made in soil for seed sowing or planting out seedlings.

Drupe A soft fleshy fruit containing one or more seeds. Drupes can also be called 'stone fruits'.

F1 hybrids Applied to the seeds of certain annuals and vegetables, these are hybrids produced by crossing selected parents that have both been inbred to produce a strain of considerable uniformity.

F2 hybrids Hybrids produced from self- or cross-pollinated F1 plants.

Farmyard manure Manure of horses, sheep and cattle, applied to soil as an improver. Poultry manures are higher in nitrogen (*see* fertiliser) and should be used with caution as they can burn young plant material.

Fertilisation The process by which a pollen grain (male) fuses with an ovule (female) to produce a fertile seed.

Fertiliser A product applied to plants to boost growth. General-purpose fertilisers usually contain equal parts of the three main nutrients required for plant growth: nitrogen, potassium and phosphorus. Use a nitrogen-high fertiliser to boost leafy growth, a potassium-high fertiliser to boost flowering and fruiting.

Fruit The ripe ovary of a plant, containing one or more seeds. Hence all seed cases can be referred to as fruits.

Garden compost A mix of decayed raw organic matter – old plant material, uncooked kitchen waste, paper and cardboard, etc – used as a soil improver. It is unsuitable as a seed or potting compost.

Germination The physiological and structural changes that occur when a seed starts into growth.

Grit *See* horticultural grit.

Growing bag A long, narrow plastic bag filled with (usually) peat-based compost and intended for growing annual crops such as tomatoes, aubergines and sweet peppers. Holes are cut in the upper surface of the bag into which young plants can be inserted.

Growing on The period between germination and planting out. Once germinated, seedlings should be kept growing strongly with good levels of light and regular watering and feeding.

Hardening off The process by which young plants are acclimatised to conditions outside the propagation unit. This generally involves removing covers from propagation units and/or placing the plants outside for increasingly longer periods.

Horticultural fleece A lightweight fabric that can be placed over young plants grown in the open ground to protect them from frost. It can also be used as a barrier against certain pests.

Horticultural grit Small stone fragments added to potting composts to improve drainage or used as a topdressing.

Hybrid A plant that has been produced by crossing two genetically distinct parents. Plants of hybrid origin cannot be reproduced from seed.

Leguminous Describing any plant of the family Leguminosae, characterised by producing seeds in pods.

Line out To plant out seedlings in a nursery bed or vegetable plot. When lining out, allow adequate space between plants for growth.

Long tom A container designed specifically for seeds that develop long roots and/or resent root disturbance.

Module A small container or growing unit used for raising seedlings. They are particularly useful for seed that can be sown individually as there is no need for pricking out and root disturbance when potting on can be minimised.

Perlite An expanded volcanic material used as an alternative to grit in potting composts.

Pod The seed case of a leguminous plant.

Pollination The transfer of pollen grains from an anther to a stigma, resulting in fertilisation.

Polytunnel A structure for protecting young plants grown outdoors, usually comprising a sheet of clear plastic stretched over a series of metal arches.

Pome A fruit that is firm in texture and contains a number of seeds. Apples, pears, quinces and medlars are pome fruits.

Pricking out The transfer of germinated seedlings into larger containers so as to allow space for growth.

Propagator A sealed unit used for seedling germination.

Radicle A young root.

Scarification The process by which the tough outer coat of a seed is breached to allow the embryo to take up water.

Seed A fertilised ovule containing a dormant embryonic plant.

Seedling A plant that has grown from a seed.

Selected form A form of a species that has arisen in gardens.

Sharp sand Sand with particles that have angular edges. It is added to potting composts to improve drainage.

Species Any plant that occurs in the wild.

Spore The reproductive structure, analogous to seed, of certain primitive, non-flowering plants such as ferns.

Stigma The part of the flower that receives the pollen.

Stratification The exposure of seeds to cold or, more rarely, warmth in order to break their dormancy.

Taproot A strong main root that grows down vertically.

Thinning The removal of a proportion of seedlings in a drill so that the remainder can develop fully.

Topgrowth Refers to the parts of a plant that are above ground level.

Transplanting Generally, the moving of a plant to a new location. Seedlings are transplanted either when they are large enough to handle and/or when they are sufficiently well developed to grow in their final positions.

Vermiculite A lightweight, expanded mineral that is used as an alternative to grit in potting composts.

Viable As applied to a seed, capable of germinating.

Seedling problems

Slugs and snails Molluscs attack the seedlings of all plants. Poisonous baits can be used but for seedlings in containers, a physical barrier usually provides better control. Keep plants under cover, in a cold frame or in a greenhouse. Regularly check for any sign of the molluscs and dispose of them by hand. In a vegetable garden, use a parasitic nematode that is watered around the plants (effective only on slugs).

Vine weevil A pest that favours pot plants. Adult females lay their eggs around plants, and the emerging grubs tunnel downwards to feed on plant roots. The most effective control is a parasitic nematode, either *Heterorhabditis megidis* or *Steinernema carpocapsae*. When potting on, check carefully for grubs. Flush out any eggs under running water and repot in fresh compost.

Damping off Caused by fungi that proliferate in damp environments, commonly on autumn and early spring sowings. Clean pots thoroughly before sowing and use fresh compost. Monitor humidity levels around seedlings. Regularly remove and wipe down the lids of propagating cases with a cloth soaked in a fungicide. Spray seedlings with the same solution.

Index

Page numbers in *italic* refer to the illustrations.

Acknowledgments

This book would not have been possible had not the following friends, neighbours and colleagues allowed me to plunder their gardens of seeds and young plants for photography. In no particular order they are: Rachel Cole, Ian and Wendy Hall, Ruth Paterson, Jack and Dorothy Hobbs, Bert and Peggy Norris, Margaret Montgomery, Matt and Sue Kinross, George Drye, estate manager at Lamport Hall, Chris and Catherine Baldwin and Jonathan and Martha Pinsent.

Nick Bolshaw at Haxnicks and Peter Powell at Parasene kindly supplied the equipment that allowed me to germinate and grow on the plants for photography. I am also indebted to Valerie Berry, who allowed Deirdre and myself to use her flat as a studio for photography.

Finally, thanks are due as always to my publisher Catie Ziller, editor Claire Musters and designer Helen McTeer, who between them had the vision and the application to see the book through from start to finish.

This book is dedicated to Finetta.

Publisher Catie Ziller
Editor Claire Musters
Designer Helen McTeer